CITIES
THEN & NOW

CITIES
THEN & NOW

JIM ANTONIOU

CHARTWELL
BOOKS, INC.

A QUARTO BOOK

Published in 1999 by Chartwell Books
A division of Book Sales, Inc.
114 Northfield Avenue
Edison, New Jersey 08837

ISBN 0-7858-1115-X

This book was designed and produced by
Quarto Publishing plc
The Old Brewery
6 Blundell Street
London N7 9BH

SENIOR EDITORS Cathy Meeus and Ellen Sarewitz
COPY EDITOR Ralph Hancock
SENIOR ART EDITOR Mark Stevens
DESIGN Peter Bridgewater and Chris Dymond
RECONSTRUCTIONS Kevin Maddison, Kevin Jones Associates,
Lawrence Taylor and Janos Marffy
MAPS Vana Haggerty
PICTURE RESEARCH Susannah Jayes and Anne-Marie Ehrlich
PICTURE MANAGER Giulia Hetherington
EDITORIAL DIRECTOR Sophie Collins
ART DIRECTOR Moira Clinch

QUAR.CIT

Typeset in Great Britain by
Central Southern Typesetters, Eastbourne
Reproduced by Eray Scan Pte. Ltd., Singapore
Printed by Winner Offset Printing Factory Ltd, China

FOR PLATON & ZOE

CONTENTS

INTRODUCTION

Civilization literally means living in a city – the word is derived from the Latin for city, *civitas*. The origin of the idea of a city was probably that of a citadel: a defensible stronghold into which people could retreat when threatened by invaders. Such a place might well be a steep, rocky hill, such as the Acropolis at Athens. Here, too, tribal gatherings would take place. A temple would be built as the focus of local religion and the leader would set up his house. In time, the citadel would become a center of administration and a permanent residence for many of its members.

The city population had to import food from outside, but would export manufactured goods to the surrounding country. Consequently, the primary function of a city became the exchange of commodities, services, and ideas.

The most suitable sites for settlements were beside watercourses, providing both drinking water and a means of communication. The beginnings of civilization lie in the valleys of the Euphrates–Tigris, the Indus, and the Nile. It would soon have become clear to the inhabitants that irrigation, flood control, and exploitation of the fertile alluvial soil could be maintained only by an elaborate communal organization.

At first, the size of a settlement seldom exceeded half a mile across – 15 minutes' leisurely walk. The distance over which water could be carried by women on foot from the local well or spring, normally about 500 feet, was also an important factor in the layout of the settlement. A further 15-minute walk out from the town gates would reach the local market gardens, or the workplaces of tradesmen such as tanners, whose malodorous work excluded them from the center.

The orientation of a settlement was also important. Sometimes climate was a factor. In the hot Asian interior, buildings and cities faced northwest, from where a cooling wind

Babylon, with its ziggurat, Hanging Gardens, and gateway dedicated to the goddess Ishtar, was the foremost city in the ancient Near East.

The Old City (top right) encompasses the most ancient remains and sacred buildings of Jerusalem.

Sanaʻa (far right) is noted for its verticality. Some 8,000 tall, narrow houses are elaborately decorated in a distinctive tracery of façades and motifs. It is on the World Heritage list.

evolved a system of subdividing towns into individual lots, based on two axial roads intersecting at right angles. The *cardo* (north–south) was often used for processions; the *decumanus* (east–west) was developed for commercial activities.

The Islamic city

Early Islamic cities were military camps called *fustats*, which were built either in the vicinity of pre-Islamic towns or completely isolated from the rest of the non-Muslim population. The fully developed Islamic city evolved gradually, with fortified walls enclosing the *jami* (main mosque) and *madrassa* (place of learning), the religious and political centers of the community. The *suq* (marketplace) was the focus of commercial and social life. The urban pattern was based on a controlled hierarchy of roads, spaces, and buildings.

The enclosed courtyard acted as the focus of home life. In some dense urban settings, such as San'a' in Yemen, the traditional courtyard house might have several storys or could even be abandoned altogether owing to lack

blew. In China, many river towns were built on south-facing slopes to receive the maximum sunshine. Mohenjodaro, capital of the ancient Indus civilization (2500–1500 B.C.) in what is now Pakistan, was laid out on a regular plan, with the principal streets running north to south, to take full advantage of the prevailing winds.

Europe in the classical era

The center of activity in a Greek *polis*, or city state, was the *agora*, or marketplace. With an increase in population and wealth, the irregular layout of the *agora* of the newly planned towns of Hellenistic times (from the mid-4th

century) began to take a more definite shape, expressing a new order in the town plan.

The late Hellenistic phase merged gradually with the Roman period. A Greco-Roman example, Pompeii, near the Bay of Naples, in Italy (latter part of the 3rd – 1st century B.C.), shows the *forum* (the Roman version of the Greek *agora*) and civic spaces composed more symmetrically than was usual in Greek town planning.

The Roman practice of town layout had its roots in military encampments or *castra* (all towns in England with names ending in "chester" were at one time Roman camps). At an early stage, the Roman land commissioners

of space or the needs of defense. The lower parts of buildings were massive, often lit only by skylights; the lighter upper parts would include an open space fulfilling the role of a courtyard.

The medieval town in Europe

The growth of commerce and trade was the chief factor in the evolution of the medieval town. Regular trade routes developed between sources and markets. Financiers and bankers remained in the town while merchants traveled abroad. The mercantile basis of urban society and its economy helped free town-dwellers from the constraints of an older rural culture.

One of the most important Western merchant cities was Venice, created by a group of refugees from Malamocco on the Adriatic coast

The Piazza del Campo, Siena, in Italy (left), is a splendid example of a medieval open space at the center of the town.

The canals of Venice (top) serve as boundaries within the city as well as interconnecting thoroughfares.

in the early 5th century. Salt pans on the small islands of the lagoons provided a lucrative export, which was exchanged for wheat with the inhabitants of neighboring areas. By the 8th century, the groups of islands were thickly populated.

Venetian trade expanded from the shores of the Adriatic Sea to Constantinople. Venetian ships traded wheat and wine from Italy, lumber from Dalmatia, and salt from the lagoons for Byzantine fabrics and Asian spices. By the 10th century, treaties of commerce had given the Venetians a privileged status in the markets of Islam, with access to all the luxuries of the Orient. Venetian buildings and the irregular narrow footpaths of the city show a strong affinity with Byzantine and Moorish forms.

From the beginning, the shallow waters of the lagoons took the place of stone walls and fortifications. Venice was divided into six *sestieri,* or neighborhoods, one for each of the six guilds of the city. Each neighborhood had its own local square, often of an odd, irregular shape, with fountains, a school, and a church.

The Grand Canal, lined with large palaces, is closely attached to the local networks of neighborhoods. The principal open space, the Piazza San Marco, evolved from marketplace to political and social center, while local trade moved out to the *sestieri.*

The central open space became an important feature of many Italian towns. The Campo of Siena, laid out in the 14th century, is adaptable to many kinds of gatherings and festivals, notably the Palio, or horserace, through the streets of the town. The broad, fan-shaped Campo is surrounded by tightly packed buildings, with access by way of a maze of narrow streets.

The influence of Renaissance design

The elements of classical civilization adopted by Renaissance Humanism changed the approach to design to a more formal one. The discovery of the principles of perspective in the 15th century altered the architect's conception of space, so that every element had to be related to the static viewpoint of the observer. The new type of street, with its imposing proportions and formal landscape, was often imposed on existing medieval forms.

Palma Nova, a Venetian town probably designed by Vincenzo Scamozzi (1552–1616), was a perfectly symmetrical spider's web of streets radiating out to the nine-sided defensive perimeter walls. The hexagonal central piazza acts as an observation post from which the streets are seen in perspective. In Sir Christopher Wren's scheme for rebuilding London after the Fire of 1666, the streets, rather than the buildings, dominate the scene.

Villas and their gardens were also designed in a single scheme. The pattern of paths found in large landscapes such as Versailles was based on the same techniques as those suggested for the layout of new towns.

Michelangelo's Piazza del Campidoglio in Rome, a fine example of a formal ensemble.

The Laws of the Indies

With the colonization of the New World, the selection of sites for settlements became a major task of exploration. As European settlers entered the Caribbean Islands, Mexico, and Central and South America in increasing numbers, Philip II of Spain in 1573 enacted the "Laws of the Indies," which established uniform standards and procedures for planning towns and their surroundings. The anonymous author of these regulations, America's first planning legislation, detailed the selection of a suitable site, the location of important buildings and spaces, and the distribution of living areas. The Laws were certainly among the most important documents in the history of urban development and influenced the layout of many North American cities.

The impact of urban growth

The social and urban changes brought by the Industrial Revolution were rapid and unprecedented. Cities were founded and doubled in size in a generation; factories, roads, canals were built, housing thrown up.

Living conditions for the working class were appalling. Every available space was built over; courts and alleys were packed, with no regard for the consequences. In some parts of Manchester, England, back-to-back houses permitted each person 35 square feet of living space, with no provision for clean water or sanitation.

The Public Health Act of 1875 set minimum standards in Britain for the width of streets and the construction, ventilation, and drainage of buildings, creating a monotony of streets and houses still seen in urban planning.

Some industrialists tried to provide better living conditions for their workers. A pioneer-

New Orleans by Landsat – a view of the city on the   *Mississippi taken at 435 miles.*

ing scheme in England was Titus Salt's model village of Saltaire, outside Bradford (1853). Other examples include the Krupp Works colony of Schederhof, Essen, in Germany (1872–3), and Pullman City, Illinois (1893). *The Garden Cities of Tomorrow* (1898), by Ebenezer Howard, offered a "healthy, natural and economic combination of town and country life" that formed the basis of many later planning techniques.

The growth of public and private transportation contributed to the expansion of suburbs. At the turn of the 20th century, more than 1 million people lived on the outskirts of New York. By 1928, 21 million motor vehicles were registered in the United States.

Other countries, where land was at a premium, developed policies for urban growth and moved urban populations to new towns. Sir Patrick Abercrombie's 1944 plan for London proposed rehousing 500,000 people.

New cities – new challenges

The years after World War II saw a period of renewed urban development. Brazil built a new capital, Brasilia, planned by Luicio Costa and designed by Oscar Niemeyer. Tokyo,

London, and New York have achieved the status of "world cities," becoming centers of political, financial, and commercial activity.

The trend increasingly is for cities to become sprawling conurbations. While the developed world is preoccupied with increasing urban amenities, cities such as Bogotá, Bombay, and Cairo are facing a different set of priorities. In Cairo, some 150,000 migrants have to be accommodated annually, and nearly all the poor live in substandard, illegally constructed housing. An additional 2 million dwellings will be required by the year 2000. A new strategy is aimed at spreading populations away from the congested center.

Urban growth is such that neighboring metropolitan cities are approaching each other along major transportation arteries to form a megalopolis, as evidenced along both coasts of the U.S.A. The Channel Tunnel is linking the heartland of Europe – London, Paris, Amsterdam, and the Ruhr valley.

Indeed, planning activity now extends beyond national boundaries, requiring co-ordination and urban management on a vast scale. At the same time, there are increasing pressures to retain the identities of individual cities through careful policies of conservation and rehabilitation.

The city scapes

The 18 cities described in this book demonstrate the qualities and failings inherent in the process or urbanization. They deal with the sequence of development from the early beginnings of commercial organization and the emergence of culture in Athens and Rome, to the rapid growth of metropolitan cities such as London, Paris, New York, Hong Kong, and Tokyo. Washington D.C., laid out as a capital for a new and powerful nation, conveys the dynamic force of city development, from a clear site to a powerful government center through the process of urban design.

Other cities such as Prague, Florence, and Jerusalem have resisted the full impact of dramatic change in their centers and have retained the traditional qualities of human

Access by car (right) requires traffic architecture on a scale not envisioned at the beginning of the 20th century.

View from the Citadel (left) shows the massive expansion of Cairo, now the largest urban center in Africa.

scale. Others still, such as Mexico City, Istanbul, and Moscow, have a glorious past, but are now coping with unprecedented urban problems. Such cities have scarce resources to deal with the needs of modern development. Relatively new cities such as Sydney and San Francisco have taken advantage of excellent locations, contributing to the quality of life for their multicultural citizens.

Yet all convey the powerful process of design and development of cities in many parts of the world. In describing these cityscapes, the dramatic contrast becomes apparent between what they must have been like at a significant early stage in their history and their present state of growth and change.

ATHENS

Here, in the city sacred to the Goddess of Wisdom, 2,500 years ago democracy was born.

An owl, symbol of the goddess Athene.

Athens was the heart of the Golden Age of Greece. The city-state clustered around the Acropolis, a rocky hill crowned with some of the most beautiful buildings the world has ever seen. On the lower slopes was the Agora, an open space used for trade and for the exercise of that Athenian invention, democracy. Since that time, Athens has grown, contracted, and grown again during foreign occupation and eventual freedom. Today it is a sprawling metropolis, choked by motor traffic and the notorious *nefos,* smog, but teeming with life and vigor.

The leading light of Europe

Although the Acropolis has been inhabited since approximately 3000 B.C. the city itself did not develop until around 1300, when Theseus united the *demes* (townships) of Attica under the leadership of Athens. The fortification of the Acropolis took place during his time, after which the city spread northwest as far as the hill of Areopagus, to cover an area which became known as the Agora of Theseus. A wall may have enclosed the city, but no traces of it have been found. Some centuries later, during the time of Solon the Lawgiver (640–560 B.C.), a program of public building was carried out which included the expansion of the Agora on the north slopes of the Acropolis.

At this time, the Acropolis was the spiritual center of Athens, crowned by the shrine of the city's goddess Athene, while the Agora below was the center of political, social, and commercial life. This division became even more obvious after the Persian Wars (490–479 B.C.)

The Erechtheion, on the north side of the Acropolis, features a porch of maidens and is unusual in being asymmetrical and on two levels.

KEY

⬜ *Themistoclean walls 480 - 350 B.C.*

⬛ *Extent in late Roman times*

⬜ *Extent at time of the Ottoman occupation, 15th to 17th centuries*

⬜ *Extent of grid plan for Athens, 1830*

⬜ *Reconstruction area*

❶ *Acropolis*
❷ *Parthenon*
❸ *Plaka*
❹ *Agora*
❺ *Propylaea*
❻ *Athens University*
❼ *Sintagmatos Square*

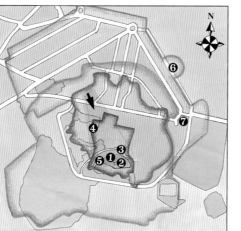

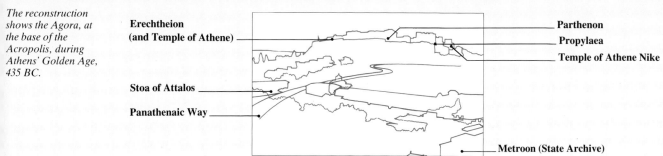

The reconstruction shows the Agora, at the base of the Acropolis, during Athens' Golden Age, 435 BC.

Erechtheion (and Temple of Athene)

Parthenon

Propylaea

Temple of Athene Nike

Stoa of Attalos

Panathenaic Way

Metroon (State Archive)

ATHENS UNDER PERICLES

The Athenian Golden Age began with the defeat of the Persians in 479 B.C. and ended with the outbreak of the Peloponnesian War in 431 B.C. For most of this time, the Athenian democracy was dominated by the great statesman, Pericles. He had a vision of Athens graced with magnificent buildings on the Acropolis and persuaded the Assembly to make annual grants of money for the work.

The Propylaea is a majestic gateway leading to the sacred rock of the Acropolis. Of the many fine buildings on the Acropolis itself, including the exquisite temple of Athene Nike and the asymmetrical Erechtheion, the most magnificent is the Parthenon.

The Parthenon, in bold Doric simplicity, was dedicated solely to Athene, the Goddess of Wisdom. It was started in 447 B.C. and completed five years later. Its architects, Ictinus and Callicrates, working with the sculptor Phidias, used a delicate marble from Mount Pentelicus, near Athens. The building was ornamented with sculptures that represent the peak of Greek art. Regarded as the most perfect of all buildings, it has not a single straight line – every part, even the pavement, is slightly curved to enhance its proportions. The immense structure dominates the city and can be seen from far out to sea, a symbol of the ancient power of Athens.

Pericles, shown in his war helmet, envisaged a city of splendid architecture paid for by annual grants from the city's allies. He called Athens "an education to Greece."

The refinement of the Acropolis was unsurpassed in classical architecture. The Propylaea fronted a series of temples culminating in the Parthenon.

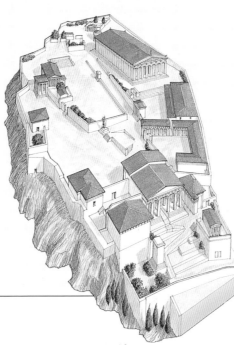

A Byzantine church of brick and stonework.

when the Persians sacked the city. Following the Athenian victory, Themistocles, the great general and statesman, built a fortification wall around the city, after which the Acropolis was no longer used as a citadel. The Parthenon, a huge temple to Athene, was built in white marble at the top of the Acropolis.

Inside its walls, ancient Athens was probably more like a large village than a capital city. Spacious parks and gardens belonging to the philosophical schools and gymnasia (schools established in the 6th century B.C. for military and athletic training), were all located outside the city walls. The city had no clear street plan. This was a defensive tactic to confuse the enemy if ever he succeeded in penetrating the city walls. The streets were owned and maintained by the city.

Rome and Byzantium

After the disastrous Peloponnesian War (431–404 B.C.) the political power of Athens declined. In 146, it fell under Roman rule. The Romans treated the city with respect, re-

On the northeastern slopes of the Acropolis are houses and churches built by the people of the island of Anaphis.

city with respect, regarding Greece and particularly Athens as the cradle of civilization, and raised new and magnificent buildings. In A.D. 267, the Herulians set fire to the city. After this, a less extensive city wall was built to the north of the Acropolis, using material from the ruins.

Athens began to grow more prosperous after the establishment of the Eastern Roman imperial capital at Constantinople in 330. Its educational and cultural institutions once again became famous, and the city expanded beyond the late Roman fortification wall until 529, when the Emperor Justinian closed the philosophical schools of Athens and the city was reduced to an unimportant town in the Byzantine Empire. In 1311, Athens became a Catalan possession until 1387 when Nerio

Acciaiuoli, the Florentine lord of Corinth, captured the city.

The last duke of Athens, Franco Acciaiuoli, surrendered the Acropolis to the Turks in 1458. They settled on the Acropolis and barred Christians. At the beginning of the Turkish occupation, the city was divided into eight areas known as *platomata*. The periphery of each *platoma* was formed by a wall of houses facing inward which could be closed off to form a secure defensive unit. These subdivisions gradually developed into neighborhoods. In turn, these were divided into parishes grouped around the local church. Turkish mosques and minarets considerably altered the skyline. The Turks transformed some existing buildings into mosques, including the Parthenon, to which they added a minaret.

The urban expansion after the arrival of the Turks was interrupted in 1687 by war with the Venetians, during which the Parthenon was partly destroyed when a cannonball ignited the munitions stored there. After two weeks of siege, the Turks abandoned Athens, which was then occupied for five months by the

Venetians. In April 1688, the Venetians left Athens after an outbreak of plague. The city remained uninhabited for three years.

On their return to Athens, the Turks fortified the city, and the fabric of urban Athens changed considerably. Plaka, to the north of the Acropolis, became the central commercial section of the city. However, the streets of residential Athens remained as narrow as they had always been. The houses were usually built with a courtyard, and privacy was guaranteed by having few or no windows in the walls facing the street.

Free again

In February 1830, Greece won recognition as an independent kingdom, and the last Turkish troops surrendered in April 1833. In September 1834, Athens was officially declared the capital of Greece. At this time, the population of the city was only 4,000, considerably less than during the classical period, when it had reached 36,000.

The overwhelming German influence in the planning of post-independence Athens meant that the revival of classical architecture in Greece arose not from the indigenous examples of classical antiquity, but from the neo-classical style which was then fashionable in Europe. There are many fine examples of such buildings in Athens, notably the University on Panepistemiou Street, built in 1839–40 to a design by Christian Hansen.

In the 20th century, especially after World War II, Athens spread rapidly and with little control, although pockets of an agreeable and pleasant environment remain, and efforts for improvement continue. Today Greater Athens, with a population of over 4 million, accommodates more than 50 percent of the country's population.

The Clock of Andronitos (1st century B.C.) is also known as the Tower of the Winds because these are shown on its frieze.

ROME

In the city of emperors and popes, the center of the world for centuries, the past seems like yesterday.

In the center of Rome at every corner, there is a column, a wall, a stretch of paving dating from the city's Imperial past. History is so close at hand that it no longer seems remote. Among these magnificent remains are crowded a fine Renaissance city and an ordinary, bustling, noisy modern one. Today's inhabitants take their past casually, living in classical apartment buildings overlooking the Trajan Forum, driving their Fiats over Roman paving stones on the Via Appia, and going to the opera in the 1,800-year-old Baths of Caracalla outside the city.

The Piazza del Campidoglio, designed by Michelangelo, heralded the arrival of the Baroque on the Capitoline Hill. He added splendid façades to the existing medieval buildings, creating a magnificent unified effect.

Capital of an Empire

Rome has been a city for nearly 3,000 years. Its early history falls into three distinctive phases. During the first phase (753–510 B.C.), Rome was ruled by kings. In the second phase (509–27 B.C.), it became a republic. In the last phase (from 27 B.C. to A.D. 330), Imperial Rome flourished as the capital of the Empire until the Emperor Constantine abandoned the city and moved the capital to Byzantium.

The earliest settlement was probably a shepherds' village on an isolated, easily defended hill close to the river Tiber. This mound, called the Palatine Hill, was one of seven hills which lay on the eastern side of the swampy valley. The settlement, with its cemetery at the bottom of the hill (where later the Roman Forum was built), was inhabited from 800 B.C. or earlier.

Rome is said to have been established and walled in 753 B.C. by Romulus, who became its first king. Certainly, from about 575 B.C., Rome was a unified city ruled by a dynasty of Etruscan princes, the Tarquinii. The city's

KEY

▫ *Palatine Hill site 750 B.C.*

▫ *The Republican Wall 350 B.C.*

▫ *The Aurelian Wall A.D. 280*

▫ *Medieval Rome 1200*

▫ *Baroque Rome 1600*

▫ *Reconstruction area*

❶ *Pantheon*
❷ *Roman Forum*
❸ *Colosseum*

❹ *Campidoglio*
❺ *St. Peter's Basilica*
❻ *Vatican City*

❼ *Piazza di Spagna*

0	Km	2
0	Mi	1

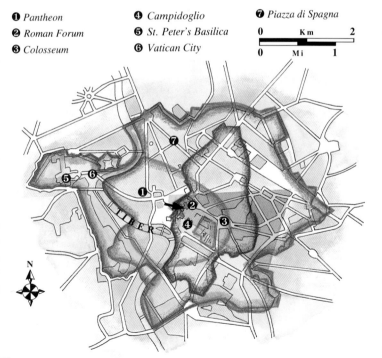

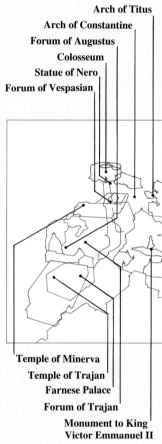

The reconstruction shows Imperial Rome during the reign of Augustus (27 BC–AD 14): the Forum and the Colosseum.

Arch of Titus
Arch of Constantine
Forum of Augustus
Colosseum
Statue of Nero
Forum of Vespasian

Temple of Minerva
Temple of Trajan
Farnese Palace
Forum of Trajan
Monument to King Victor Emmanuel II

fortifications were strengthened, and swamps were drained by canals, thus making the site of the Forum habitable. On the Capitoline Hill, a temple to Jupiter was erected as a symbol of Rome's unity.

In 510 B.C., the Romans ousted the monarchy and established a republic. By the beginning of the 4th century B.C., Rome was the leading city in central Italy. Its armies conquered first the neighboring tribes, then in 202 B.C., defeated the invading Carthaginians and annexed their colonies in Spain. In 146, the Romans gained power in Greece; in 133, they took on much of Asia Minor. The Roman Empire grew steadily – though not without reverses. In 390 B.C., the Gauls briefly took the city of Rome itself, but were soon ejected.

Rome did not follow any particular rules of city planning. The terrain of seven hills was not an easy site to develop in a systematic way. Moreover, there was little control in accommodating an ever-increasing population. By the 1st century A.D., Rome had become a monstrous muddle. In the towns built in their foreign dominions, the Romans used an admirably clear grid plan centered on two main streets forming a cross (the north–south *cardo* and the east–west *decumanus*). In their own city, the chance to do that was long since gone. But the Romans had never lacked the ability to organize, and they kept their capital functioning.

Two basic needs had to be met: a growing number of inhabitants had to be housed, and adequate public services such as water supply and the disposal of waste had to be provided. The Romans solved their civil engineering problems with typical panache. One of their most important inventions was a superior concrete made from pozzolana, a sandy mineral, mixed with lime. Most of their build-

LIVING IN AN INSULA

The city, unable to expand sideways on its hilly site, grew upward into apartment bluildings called *insulae*, with as many as five storys. An *insula* had about five apartments or *cericulae,* each housing five or six persons. *Insulae,* usually poorly constructed, often collapsed. For this reason, Julius Caesar limited their height to 70 feet, later reduced to 60 feet by Trajan. Rents were high and tenants

Insulae enabled people to live close to the center of the city.

sublet rooms, leading to overcrowding.

Water was supplied only to the rich and to those who occupied the ground floor of each *insula* – either shops or single tenants who could afford the rents. The rest of the population used water from public fountains.

ings, however, were of brick. In their grand buildings, these materials were faced with stone. The concrete dome of the Pantheon, built in the first century A.D., is almost 150 feet in diameter – unequaled until the building of St. Peter's in the same city 15 centuries later.

There were two principal types of housing: the *domus*, a group of rooms around a courtyard, and the *insula*, an apartment building. Surveys made in the 4th century A.D. show that there were almost 1,800 *domus*-type houses and some 46,600 *insulae* scattered around in almost every part of the city, well-to-do families living next to poor people in cramped apartments. The nobility also had luxurious villas outside the walls.

The swampy ground in the Tiber valley was drained, streams were covered over, and channels dug. The first main sewer, the Cloaca Maxima, was constructed as early as 578 B.C.

The Cloaca Maxima (left) was Rome's first major sewer, built more than 2,500 years ago. Parts of it are still in use.

The Colosseum is a vast ellipse with seating for 50,000 spectators around the central arena.

and was vaulted over in 184 B.C.

The Tiber supplied water until the volume of sewage discharged in the river made it undrinkable. A vast system of elevated aqueducts was built to bring clean water into the city from the surrounding hills. These had to be made extremely tall to serve the highest parts of the hilly city. A total of 316 miles was eventually built, carrying 200 million gallons of water daily.

During the 2nd century A.D., the population of Rome reached 1.2 million. Records show that by the 3rd century there were 247 reservoirs, with 11 major *thermae* (large public baths), more than 900 other public baths, and over 1,200 public fountains. Permission to build a new private bath was restricted to those who could arrange an adequate water supply for themselves. Water from the aqueducts was metered through narrow nozzles with an official seal to prevent tampering.

The public places were embellished with magnificent temples and public buildings on the grandest possible scale, set around several large forums linked by broad streets. In A.D. 64, a fire destroyed large parts of the most crowded areas of the city. This allowed the Emperor Nero to redevelop the city center in a more spacious style. Over the centuries, the city walls were rebuilt seven times.

The center of Rome

The oldest parts of the city, on the Palatine and Capitoline hills, remained at the center as the city expanded to accommodate a growing population. Development was restricted by the terrain and by the sacred nature of particular sites. Over 150 years, a mosaic of buildings emerged, from the vast Colosseum in the southeast of the central area to the Temple of Trajan in the northwest.

The most prominent of these structures was the Forum. This was a central space used as a meeting place, a market, and a political center. The oldest and most important was the Roman Forum. The principal public buildings, including the Senate House and the immense, domed Basilica of Maxentius, were built around it.

Several forums were built by succeeding emperors, from 33 B.C. to A.D. 114. The first of the new forums was that of Julius Caesar, followed by the Forum of Augustus, who became the first Roman emperor (27 B.C.–A.D. 14). The Forum of Vespasian functioned as a public library. Between it and the Forum of Augustus was the Forum of Nerva. The last and most impressive forum was built by Trajan (98–117).

The center of Rome developed into a sequence of groups of public buildings, of

ever-increasing size and magnificence.

Decline and fall

Rome's Golden Age lasted from the reign of Augustus to a few decades beyond. After the reign of Emperor Trajan, Rome's splendor began to diminish. As early as A.D. 9, when the Roman general Varus had been routed by an army of Germans under Arminius, the Empire had begun to look unstable.

In 330, Constantine, the first Christian emperor, divided the Empire in two and transferred the Imperial administration to Constantinople. In 407, with Rome increasingly under attack, the Western capital was transferred to Ravenna. In 410, Rome fell to the Goths. Increasingly weak puppet emperors reigned briefly. In 476, Theodoric, King of the Ostrogoths, with the permission of the Eastern Emperor Zeno, captured Rome and set himself up as Western Emperor. Under his rule the Empire enjoyed a final brief Indian summer.

Papal Rome

But a new power was rising – that of the Church. Rome had been the center of Western Christendom since the time of Constantine. Now, no longer a secular capital, it became a religious one, the goal of pilgrimages from all parts of Europe. Jubilees, organized to raise funds and promote the authority of the Church, attracted some 2 million pilgrims a year.

By now, the city had shrunk to a small town. During much of the Middle Ages, the population was no more than 30,000. The classical buildings, already wrecked by barbarian invasions, were being dismantled and their stones burned to make lime. Most of the population was crowded into a small riverside quarter near the Castel Sant' Angelo, a medieval fort built on a Roman mausoleum.

The Renaissance in Rome began with Pope Nicolas V (1447–55), who saw the embellishment of the city with majestic buildings as a stable and convincing way of passing on the Christian faith. He also played a positive role in extending hospitality to the artists and intellectuals who fled to Rome when Constantinople fell to the Turks in 1453.

The Rome of Pope Sixtus V

In the five years (1585–90) of Sixtus' papacy, he replanned the city based on a system of "nodes" – central points which were the sites of ancient buildings, churches, captured Egyptian obelisks and columns. Between these ran new avenues, widening into spacious squares. The Pope himself walked the streets to experience the distance between nodes.

The plan reduced the apparent distances between parts of the expanding city. For example, the distance along the Strada Felice from the Porta del Popolo to the church of Santa Croce in Gerusalemme was some 2.6 miles, and the street was planned to be wide enough to allow five carriages to travel abreast. Although the portion from the Porta del Popolo to Santa Trinità dei Monti was never actually built, the entire distance was broken down visually by a series of monuments situated along the thoroughfare.

Domenico Fontana, the Pope's right-hand

VATICAN CITY

An enclave within Rome, Vatican City is the smallest country in the world, covering about 109 acres. This city within a city on the west bank of the Tiber is dominated by St. Peter's Basilica (built 1506–26) and its huge circular colonnaded piazza by Bernini, located in the southeastern corner. St. Peter's, the largest church in the world, was partly designed by Michelangelo. Bernini's original plan was for a sequence of three spaces leading from the church: the Piazza Retta, immediately in front; the large Piazza Obliqua, embraced by the colonnades and incorporating the central obelisk erected by Sixtus V in 1586; and the Piazza Rustiucci – never completed.

Through this sumptuous sequence of movement, the Vatican shows extraordinary faith in the power of urban

The lavish complex of the Vatican, seen here from the air, was created without regard for expense.

design, equal to that of Imperial Rome, intended to reflect the glories of the Church and the primacy of ecclesiastical authority over the princes of the earth.

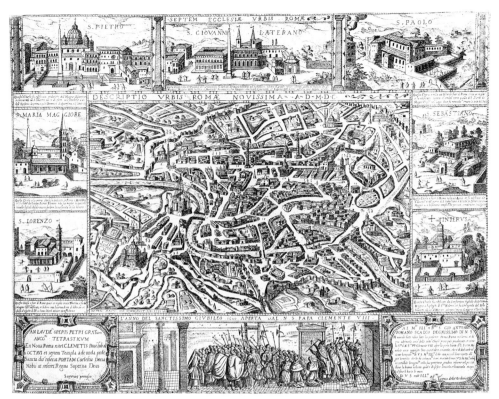

The powerful scheme of Pope Sixtus V turned the disorderly medieval city of Rome into a fitting capital of Christendom.

and the city was quickly surrounded with un-attractive new suburbs, including some 600,000 illegally built houses. The 1960 Olympics were held in Rome, which added some fine sports facilities. From the 1970s, inconclusive attempts were made to deal with the city's poor public housing and acute traffic congestion. These have culminated in a ban on motor traffic in much of the city center.

The Scala de Spagna, (1721–5), by Alessandro Specchi and Francesco de Santis, acts as a three-dimensional public square.

man, was able to remark: "One can by foot, by horse, or in a carriage, start from whatever place in Rome one may wish and continue virtually in a straight line to the most famous devotions." Some 1,300 years after Classical Rome, the city was once more one of the great sights of the world.

Modern Rome

When Rome became the capital of a unified Italy in 1870, it was no more extensive than a provincial town. Soon plans were put in hand to enlarge it and give it the status of a national capital. Heavy industry was kept away from the city, while the area around the Termini and the new Piazza Vittorio Emanuele were planned as the home of the civil service. The Piazza itself was ornamented with a huge monument to King Victor Emmanuel II in an astonishing wedding-cake style. New suburbs were laid out along main roads such as the Via Veneto and Via Nazionale.

These grandiose schemes made a conscious effort to isolate the Pope, whose territories beyond the Vatican had been annexed by the new state. The broad avenues ran past the Vatican as if it did not exist.

But these were eclipsed by Mussolini's spacious network of streets and squares planned for the city center in the 1920s, to the despair of archaeologists.

After the war, the Italian economy boomed

ISTANBUL

Capital of half an empire, Byzantium, or Antoninia, or Constantinople, or Istanbul, has always been a place in the middle of things.

Standing at the junction of two continents and two seas, Constantinople was the greatest city in the world for many centuries. It was a bridge between two cultures in more ways than one. The Byzantine Empire, ruled from this city, preserved the learning of the ancient world and passed it on to the modern era. The great church of Hagia Sophia, crowned by an immense dome, was a feat of engineering unrivaled for almost a thousand years. Today Constantinople has become Istanbul, a unique mixture of ancient and modern, of East and West.

Byzantium

Around 660 B.C., on a pleasant peninsula on the southwestern side of the Bosphorus with a fine natural harbor to the north, Megarian Greek settlers founded a city named after their leader Byzas. From about 150 B.C., Byzantium became a free city paying tribute to Rome until after A.D. 70, when the Emperor Vespasian absorbed Byzantium into the Roman Empire.

During the 2nd century A.D. Byzantium supported an unsuccessful candidate in the struggle for imperial power. The final victor, Septimus Severus, showed his displeasure by capturing the city in 196 and burning it to the ground. However, Severus realized the importance of such a strategic location, linking Europe with Asia and, through the Sea of Marmara, the Mediterranean with the Black Sea. He added new fortifications and enlarged the city, naming it Antoninia.

Once more the citizens backed the wrong man when the pagan Licinius became an imperial candidate against Constantine. On becoming Emperor, Constantine captured

Today Constantinople is named Istanbul, from the Greek eis tēn polin, meaning "to the city." This early print shows a street scene with a Turkish water fountain.

The promontory at the mouth of the Bosphorus made Constantinople a self-contained fortress.

KEY

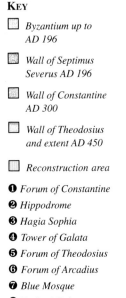

☐ *Byzantium up to AD 196*

▨ *Wall of Septimus Severus AD 196*

▨ *Wall of Constantine AD 300*

☐ *Wall of Theodosius and extent AD 450*

☐ *Reconstruction area*

❶ *Forum of Constantine*
❷ *Hippodrome*
❸ *Hagia Sophia*
❹ *Tower of Galata*
❺ *Forum of Theodosius*
❻ *Forum of Arcadius*
❼ *Blue Mosque*
❽ *Topkapi Palace*

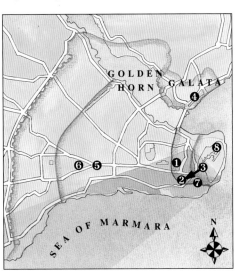

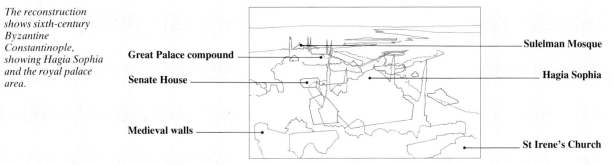

The reconstruction shows sixth-century Byzantine Constantinople, showing Hagia Sophia and the royal palace area.

Great Palace compound

Senate House

Medieval walls

Sulelman Mosque

Hagia Sophia

St Irene's Church

29

FROM WALLED SETTLEMENT TO FORTIFIED CITY

From its early beginnings, the small settlement of Byzantium grew steadily westward, starting from the tip of the peninsula and then during its time as Antoninia, spreading up to the walls of Septimus Severus. Constantine built his fortifications some 2 miles west of the Severian wall in A.D. 330.

In 413 Theodosius II, fearing an invasion by Attila the Hun, extended the fortifications – and thus the city itself – to the west by about 1 mile. A moat 60 feet wide and 20 feet deep formed the first defense, in front of a 15-foot high outer wall where troops could assemble. The main rampart walls 15 feet thick and 40 feet high on the outside, were protected by 100 towers 60 feet high. These ramparts were so powerfully built that they survived for more than 1,000 years (only once successfully attacked, by the Fourth Crusaders), until finally breached by Turkish cannon in 1453. Up to the middle of the 19th century, Constantinople

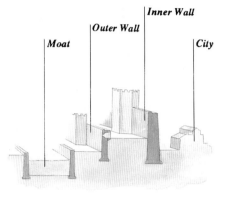

The great wall ran from the Sea of Marmara to the Golden Horn.

remained within the 13-mile long wall of Theodosius.

The emperors also built massive palaces outside the walls, one chronicler remarking that these were as large as cities. Across the Golden Horn to the north were the fortified colony of Galata, where the Genoese lived; and Pera, the European quarter.

Constantine I adopted Christianity as the Empire's religion.

the new capital.

Constantinople adopted the two-headed eagle as its emblem. It signified that the new order was powerful enough to look to the East and to the West, and that the Empire was both aware of past achievements and committed to a glorious future.

Little is known of the early layout of Constantinople, when the emperors were rarely in residence. Like Rome, it was built on seven hills (a common claim by cities with aspirations to greatness). The city was divided into 14 districts, linked by a system of main roads and with well-organized civic spaces and public buildings, including the circular Forum of Constantine. In contrast to the ordered public places, residential districts grew haphazardly.

The city was always heavily populated, and much of the early development was lost to subsequent rebuilding. Only the column bearing Constantine's statue survives from that early period.

Antoninia, but again he realized that the city was too strategically important to destroy.

The city of Constantine

The decline of Rome and the gradual breakdown of the pagan system of state religion encouraged Constantine to adopt Christianity as the official religion. He was also keen to found a new capital away from the constant pressures and threats of the western side of the Empire. In 330, he chose Byzantium as the site for the new capital, which he named Constantinopolis. He urged people of influence in the Empire to settle there. Some were offered palaces and encouraged to contribute to the building of the city, while others were given large estates outside the walls so that they might take an active part in the growth of

LIFE IN CONSTANTINOPLE

From Constantinople, the West learned the art of diplomacy and borrowed from the imperious and formal style of painting. The city's architects, through the ingenious device of the pendentive, refined the method of building a large dome on a square base. All the Greek literature which has survived to the present at some point passed through Constantinople.

Through the city's 1100 years of turbulent history, the Byzantine Empire was ruled by 88 Emperors, starting with Constantine I and ending with Constantine XI. Many Emperors died violently, others quietly in monasteries.

Today, Constantinople is named Istanbul, but even this is a Greek name, from *eis tēn polin,* meaning "to the city." It remains a fascinating city of contrasts, where vendors who would seem at home in the Dark Ages stand amid the teeming traffic. The finest modern architecture in Turkey jostles with a labyrinth of colorful bazaars. A jagged skyline of domes and minarets is interrupted by the towers of international hotels.

As Rome declined and fell Constantinople prospered and grew, becoming the focus of the civilized world for eleven centuries. Between the 6th and 11th centuries, the fortified city accommodated some half a million people, providing free medical services and assistance to the destitute. Trades were organized into official guilds, and contractors were required to replace faulty

Today Istanbul is a city of contrasts, where buildings of a bygone age stand next to modern structures amid the teeming traffic.

work as a matter of course. There were also housing codes which controlled construction and the extent of balconies over streets. Little distinction was made between ethnic groups and nationalities. However, adherence to Orthodox Christianity (as the official state religion) and, from the 7th century on, the ability to speak Greek, became the requisites for social acceptability.

Visitors from medieval Europe were surprised to find such a majestic metropolis, with its busy harbor serving the markets for silk, gold, silver, and spices. At a time when Byzantine Emperors were recognized as scholars, equally skilled in diplomacy and business, many leaders in Europe could not read or write.

THE HIPPODROME

The Hippodrome was an open space, with its obelisks from the ancient world.

The Hippodrome was to Constantinople what the Colosseum had been to Rome. Chariot races were held regularly, entertaining some 60,000 spectators. At the center was the *spina,* the long wall around which the chariots raced. Along it stood statues honoring famous charioteers, together with masterpieces of classical art and monuments gathered from around the world. There was an obelisk from Egypt and the famous column of the three serpents from Delphi, commemorating the Greek victory against the Persians at the Battle of Plataea.

Here, the Emperor came in direct contact with the people. The inhabitants registered their disapprobation or approval of political and social events, often leading to riots that had to be brutally contained.

Today the Hippodrome survives as an open space. Some of the monuments that decorated the famous *spina* are still there.

The age of the Eastern Emperors

During the reign of Theodosius II (408–50), Constantinople expanded further out toward the west; new fortifications were added in 413. From that time on, the Emperors settled permanently in Constantinople.

At this time, the city was embellished with splendid buildings and elegant spaces. Around the main square, called the Augusteum, were grouped the Great Palace, the Senate House, the large public baths, and the massive Hippodrome. On the west side was the golden milestone called Milion, from which distances were measured to all parts of the Empire. From there the Mese, a large avenue lined with shops, led westward through the Forum of Constantine. The Forum of Theodosius was decorated with a massive arch, and the Forum of Arcadius contained a column 140 feet high, bearing a statue of the Emperor. Some 4 miles to the west, the avenue reached the walls of Theodosius and a triumphal arch at the Golden Gate. At the western part of the city, large open cisterns were built to maintain the water supply.

The Empire fell into bitter civil wars. Constantinople was actually sacked by the soldiers of the Fourth Crusade (1202–4). Then came a fatal struggle between the Byzantines and the Turks. On Tuesday, May 29, 1453, Constantine XI was killed, and Mehmet (Muhammad) II triumphantly entered the city which had dominated the Middle Ages.

This miniature shows astronomers observing the sky from the Galata tower.

HAGIA SOPHIA

Hagia Sophia, or the Church of Holy Wisdom, took 10,000 men five years to build. Massive arches springing 65 feet from the ground provided pendentives to support the vast dome 100 feet in diameter, rising 170 feet above the floor of the church. Outside the central core additional piers, columns, and walls provided side aisles and arcades. Despite the massiveness of the structure, the internal space has a feeling of lightness and grace.

Throughout construction Justinian took direct control of the work, visiting the site almost daily. Materials were brought from many temples in various parts of the Empire, including Rome, Athens, Delphi, and Ephesus. Walls, domes, and arches were constructed in brickwork, dressed in

The interior has a feeling of grace.

Hagia Sophia is based on a rectangle with four huge pillars forming a square.

stone and marble. The area covered by the dome is among the largest in the world.

The lower parts of the walls were covered in multicolored marble. The original mosaics that embellished the walls and dome are now entirely replaced. When Hagia Sophia was completed, on the day of its dedication, December 27, 537, Justinian was able to proudly claim, "I have conquered thee, O Solomon."

On June 1, 1473, Mehmet II removed the cross from above the dome and turned Hagia Sophia into a mosque. The precious mosaics were covered with plaster and tall minarets were added. In 1935 it was opened to the public as a museum.

Mosaic of Christ the King, 12th century, in the apse of Hagia Sophia.

JERUSALEM

*The name of this holiest of cities means "founded in peace,"
yet Jerusalem has been fought over for most
of its long history.*

Jerusalem is a sacred place for three major religions, Judaism, Christianity, and Islam. One of the longest-inhabited cities in the world, it can trace its history back some 4,000 years. Jerusalem lies on a line dividing the East from the West. Throughout its turbulent history, it has shifted from one sphere of influence to another with each successive conquest. Today it is claimed by Israel as its capital – a claim the United Nations does not recognize. Surrounded by a ring of modern development, the ancient center retains much of its stony grandeur.

A mountain stronghold

Jerusalem is sited at an ancient crossing of trade routes, on a platform sharply defined by steep slopes and deep valleys on three sides, making it easy to defend in time of war. This in turn is surrounded by rocky hills. Early settlers would have been attracted to the site by the reliable water supply from the Spring of Gihon, and the fertile soil in the Kidron Valley to the south.

Jerusalem's written history begins at the traditional date of 1451 B.C., when Joshua captured it for the Israelites from King Adoni-Zedec. Around 1000, King David established it as the capital of a united Israel, and his successor Solomon built the Temple, the principal holy place of the Jews. This stood on the Temple Mount, a natural hill which was later built up into a rectangular platform. Below this clustered narrow streets, often stepped to accommodate the steep slopes, lined with

Travelers have documented Jerusalem over many centuries. This watercolor of the city's skyline is by K.F.H. Werner.

KEY

- ☐ *Ancient cities of Solomon and David*
- ☐ *Herod Agrippa's walls in A.D. 45*
- ☐ *Extent in the 12th century A.D.*
- ☐ *Reconstruction area*

- ❶ *Dome of the Rock*
- ❷ *Second Temple*
- ❸ *Church of the Holy Sepulcher*
- ❹ *Damascus Gate*
- ❺ *Mount of Olives*
- ❻ *Mount Zion*
- ❼ *Western "Wailing" Wall*
- ❽ *The Citadel (David's Tower)*
- ❾ *Rockefeller Museum*

The reconstruction
shows the aftermath of
the First Crusade
(1099): rebuilding the
Old City and Temple
Mount 1150.

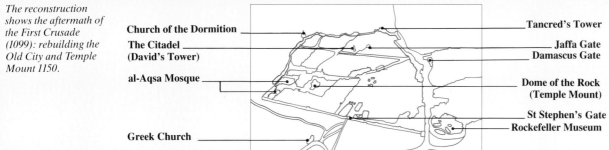

Church of the Dormition

The Citadel
(David's Tower)

al-Aqsa Mosque

Greek Church

Tancred's Tower

Jaffa Gate
Damascus Gate

Dome of the Rock
(Temple Mount)

St Stephen's Gate
Rockefeller Museum

houses built of local limestone, probably not much different in appearance from the older buildings in today's city.

In 586 Nebuchadnezzar, King of Babylon, captured and razed Jerusalem and deported the population. Cyrus allowed the Jews to return, and around 445 the walls were rebuilt. But in 333, Alexander the Great captured the city. Jerusalem was now part of the Western world, in which it was to remain for the next thousand years. When Alexander's brief conquests fell apart, Jerusalem became the property of the Hellenistic rulers of Egypt, though it was menaced by the Syrian Seleucids. Eventually, in 63 B.C., it was captured by the Roman general Pompey, and the whole of Judaea became a Roman province. A revolt by the citizens led to the complete destruction of the city by the Emperor Titus in A.D. 70.

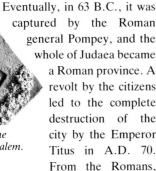

A tile denoting the Romans in Jerusalem.

From the Romans, Jerusalem passed under Byzantine rule until the Islamic conquest of 638. With the exception of a brief period when Jerusalem was retaken by the Crusaders in the 12th century, the city was now firmly under oriental influence. In 1517, it became part of the Ottoman Empire.

The British captured the city from the Turks in 1917, by which time, despite its religious importance, it had declined to little more than a provincial town. From 1948, when the State of Israel established itself, until 1967 Jerusalem was a divided city, with most of the holy places in Jordan. After the Six-Day War of 1967, Israel took over the entire city. Today Jerusalem owes its character to many ethnic groups, including Jews, Greeks, Romans, Arabs, Armenians, Turks, British, and other Europeans. All have contributed to build the holy city into a place like no other in the world.

The city of the Bible

Although Jerusalem was captured by Joshua, it was not settled by the Israelites. The city had to be retaken from the Jebusites by David around 1000 B.C. During his reign, the city covered an area of some 11 acres and was the capital of a kingdom stretching from Lebanon south into the Negev desert, and some way across the Jordan to the east.

Solomon, his successor, lost much of the territory, but building work continued apace in Jerusalem, including the Temple and Palace (about 950 B.C.), which took 20 years to complete. In Solomon's reign, Jerusalem grew to

The mount of Olives and the site of the original city of David (11 acres), were taken from the Jebusites c.1000 B.C.

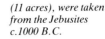

THE MADABA MAP

The earliest surviving depiction of Jerusalem.

On the floor of the Greek Orthodox Church of St. George in the small Jordanian town of Madaba is the only ancient map of Palestine in existence, a mosaic dating from A.D. 560–65. At the center is Jerusalem, represented in some detail to show the development of the city at this time. The map includes some buildings on the Temple platform, with the Golden Gate to the east side, and two colonnaded streets running south from the column set up in honor of Hadrian and Antonius Pius inside the North Gate. The façade of the Church of the Holy Sepulcher is shown facing the colonnaded *cardo*.

cover an area of 32 acres. After his death in 928, the city declined in importance until its destruction by the Babylonians in 586.

During the reign of Herod the Great, "King of the Jews" under Roman rule (37–34 B.C.), considerable building took place, including a new and much larger Temple and the platform enclosing Temple Mount, as well as various other temples and palaces, fortresses, a theater, and a hippodrome. Under Herod Agrippa I (A.D. 37–44), more construction was undertaken, enlarging the city's walls to the north and adding an imposing Triple Gate on the site of the present Damascus Gate.

The new buildings did not last long. After the Jewish revolt in 70, the city was systematically flattened. All that remained of the Temple was the lower parts of some of the walls. The Temple area remained an open space until the Islamic conquest in 638.

Aelia Capitolina

In A.D. 130, the Emperor Hadrian decided to found a new city on the ruins of Jerusalem, which he renamed *Aelia Capitolina.* It had a typical cruciform Roman layout, with one main street, the *cardo,* running south from the present Damascus Gate, and the other, the *decumanus,* extending from the west at the Jaffa Gate to the east, along David Street.

In A.D. 324, the Emperor Constantine brought Palestine under the Christian Eastern Roman Empire, and the city regained its name. During the early Byzantine period, when many churches were built, Jerusalem still followed the Roman street plan and the line of the walls.

In the same year, Macarius, Bishop of Jerusalem, gained permission to remove the Roman Temple of Venus from the site which was believed to be the tomb of Christ. Near this site Helena, mother of the Emperor Constantine, claimed to have discovered the True Cross. Constantine built the Church of the Holy Sepulcher over the sites of the Rock of Crucifixion, location of the True Cross and the Tomb. Later, the Empress Eudocia, wife of the Emperor Theodosius II, extended the city to the southern end of the Tyropoean valley.

Jerusalem became the center of Christianity and reached its peak of development during the Byzantine period under the Emperor Justinian (527–65). Within the fortified city, Justinian extended the *cardo* in a monumental layout southward to the Nea Church and Gate.

Al-Quds

In 638, Jerusalem fell to the Arabs and was renamed al-Quds. It was already a holy place for them. On the Temple Mount, Caliph Abd al-Malik built the Dome of the Rock, which was completed in 691. The adjoining al-Aqsa Mosque was rebuilt on a large scale in about 710.

The Church of the Holy Sepulcher was destroyed in a fit of rage by the ruler al-Hakim in 1009. However, many buildings were provided for the Muslim community, including mosques, gates, hospitals, and baths served by a new water supply system. The city walls were also improved in 1033 and 1063.

The Crusaders who recaptured Jerusalem in 1099 killed almost all the city's Muslims and Jews. They built numerous churches, many of which survive to this day, including a new Church of the Holy Sepulcher. The Dome of the Rock was turned into a church, while the al-Aqsa Mosque became the administrative

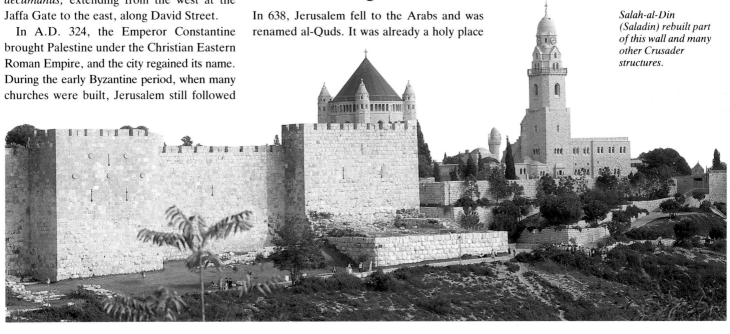

Salah-al-Din (Saladin) rebuilt part of this wall and many other Crusader structures.

base of the Crusaders. Powerful monastic orders were also established at this time, and these undertook much of the construction work. But in 1187, Salah al-Din (Saladin) retook the city for the Muslims.

Saladin rebuilt the city walls and converted many Crusader structures to Muslim use, while other buildings reverted to their original Islamic state. He also added many new buildings, of which some 24 survive to this day. Succeeding Muslim rulers of Jerusalem gave the Old City much of its present character.

During the Ottoman period (1517–1917), Suleiman the Magnificent (1494–1566) carried out considerable rebuilding. The city expanded outside the walls, and institutions were established to accommodate pilgrims from many parts of the world. The city was full of Christians and Jews who were tacitly permitted to practice their religions provided that they did not make too much public show. But as the Ottoman Empire declined, so did Jerusalem. By the mid-19th century, it was in an advanced

Salah-al-Din added many buildings, of which 24 survive. This view of eastern

Jerusalem shows the Old City, with its predominantly Islamic architecture.

THE DOME OF THE ROCK

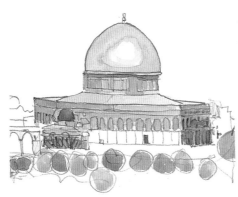

The façade of the Dome of the Rock shows the extraordinarily rich tile ornament for which it has become world famous.

The second caliph 'Umar, or Omar, who captured Jerusalem in 638, allowed Christians to retain their monuments, mainly in the northwestern quarter, but the Temple Mount remained empty. The large rock on this site is said to mark the place of Abraham's intended sacrifice of his son Isaac and of Mohammed's final flight to heaven. Here, Caliph Abd al-Malik built the Dome of the Rock, or Mosque of Omar, in 691, as a place of pilgrimage. Although heavily restored and repaired, the Dome retains the quality of the original, mathematically harmonious in its proportions and ornamented with mosaic, its dome covered in gold leaf. This octagonal building remains one of the most original examples of Islamic architecture.

state of decay. The Crimean War re-established European interest, and some repairs and new building were carried out.

Modern Jerusalem

In 1917, Palestine, and Jerusalem with it, became a British Mandate. The city expanded further, adding modern buildings to accommodate a growing population. The urban management of Jerusalem improved rapidly during this period. Administration and service buildings were provided in 1921, and the water supply was enlarged and brought up to standard. New building codes required structures to be constructed or faced with the fine local limestone to retain the city's traditional architectural character.

As Jewish immigration increased, Arab anxiety grew. There were terrorist acts by both sides against each other and the British. Eventually, war broke out. On May 14, 1948, the British left, and the following day the battle for Jerusalem began between the new State of Israel and the Arabs. The ceasefire in 1949 proposed establishing Jerusalem as an international city. In the event, it was divided in two between Israel and Jordan. For many years thereafter, the only crossing point was the famous Mandelbaum Gate – named after the original owner of the house next to it.

By the late 19th century, the city was in decay and amounted to little more than a provincial town. The British took the city from the Turks in 1917.

THE WAILING WALL

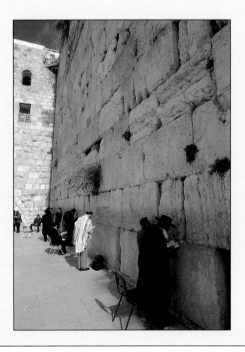

The Temple Mount occupies one-fifth of the area of the Old City and is sacred to all three religions. The original Temple of Solomon was destroyed by Nebuchadnezzar. Herod the Great enlarged the platform and rebuilt the Temple. Its destruction by Titus in A.D. 70 was thorough, but what remains has been uncovered. The massive lower courses of wall belong to Herod's Temple, while the smaller blocks above are parts of later Roman, Byzantine, and Muslim structures. The Western Wall is the most sacred for the Jews, who to this day come to mourn the destruction of Solomon's Temple. For this reason, it is commonly known as the Wailing Wall.

Jews mourn the loss of Solomon's Temple at the remains of its western wall.

Israeli claims to Jerusalem as the capital of Israel were reinforced by their capture of the eastern half of the city in the 1967 war. The Israelis promptly set about expanding it, adding a ring of ugly modern concrete developments which have disfigured the surrounding hills.

The expansion of the modern city has been balanced by restoration and conservation of the Old City. Powerful religious interests conflict as to what is to be preserved in a city where past development has taken place in layer upon layer of succeeding buildings. Jerusalem presents one of the most intractable restoration problems of any city.

FLORENCE

Brunelleschi's lofty dome, the first grand project of the Renaissance, soars over a city which has housed the world's greatest artists.

KEY

☐ *Roman settlement*

▨ *Extent up to 12th century A.D.*

▧ *14th-century walls*

☐ *Reconstruction area*

❶ *San Lorenzo*

❷ *Palazzo della Signoria (Palazzo Vecchio)*

❸ *Cathedral*

❹ *Brunelleschi's Foundling Hospital*

❺ *Piazza della Santissima Annunziata*

❻ *Uffizi*

❼ *Pitti Palace*

❽ *Ponte Vecchio*

lorence marks the transition from the Middle Ages to the Renaissance. In its medieval setting, Florence produced fragments of elegant new urban design by means of a subtle use of perspective and proportion. It passed on this novel approach to the world. The concept of the ideal city was central to the thinking of architects, artists, and philosophers. Here a first attempt was made to put the ideal into practice.

Roman Florence developed along the banks of the Arno River. Its Latin name Florentia means "flowering," a reference to the fertile Tuscan valley in which it was situated. In 90 B.C., it was granted the status of a *municipium*, or free town, but two years later it was destroyed by Sulla in a civil war.

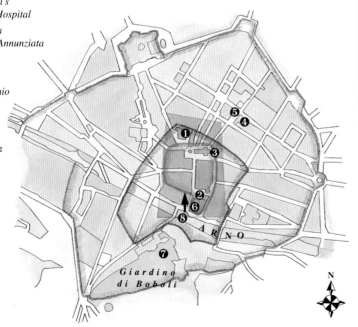

Brunelleschi's dome over the cathedral provided a focus for the planning of Florence. The city became the workshop for Early Renaissance urban design. The cathedral sits at the center of an extensive network of routes connecting major buildings and squares over most of the city.

The reconstruction shows the center of Florence in 1425, when the dome of the cathedral was being completed.

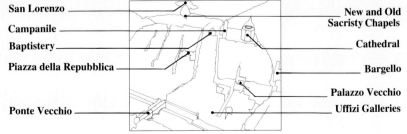

San Lorenzo

Campanile

Baptistery

Piazza della Repubblica

Ponte Vecchio

New and Old Sacristy Chapels

Cathedral

Bargello

Palazzo Vecchio

Uffizi Galleries

The Palazzo della Signoria (also called the Palazzo Vecchio), the symbol of civil power, was begun by Arnolfo di Cambio and continued after his death by Giotto.

Florentia was rebuilt as a Roman colony, occupying an area of 79 acres within its fortified walls. The two main streets crossing at right angles, characteristic of a Roman town (the *cardo* and *decumanus*), divided Florence into four districts. Some of the city's streets are still named after the original Roman buildings: the Via delle Terme, for the public baths; the Via del Campidoglio, for the city hall.

During the early Christian period, there was intensive building, and a number of churches survive from that time, such as San Lorenzo, Santa Reparata, and Santa Felicità, although Florence was sacked by barbarians several times. In 1052, it passed into the hands of Countess Matilda of Tuscany. At this time, the striking green-and-white patterned church of San Miniato al Monte was built, using marble columns from Roman ruins.

In the 12th century, a new ring of fortifications was built around the city on both sides of the Arno, enclosing 197 acres. During the 12th and 13th centuries, the population reached 60,000. The cloth industry, silk and wool, was mainly responsible for the city's economic prosperity. Rough silk from Asia and wool from England were imported through the Mediterranean ports and dyed in beautiful colors, for which the city became renowned.

A measure of Florence's economic success was the minting of the famous gold *fiorino* (florin), which became accepted currency throughout Europe. This was the basis of a successful banking system: the "letter of credit" was invented by Florentine bankers.

In 1250, the city proclaimed itself an independent *Comune* (republic). Further fortification walls were added, enclosing 1,550 acres. With frequent wars and the devastating effects of the Black Death in the 1340s, the medieval population never recovered. Florence was unable to occupy this enclosed area fully until the second half of the 19th century, when for a brief period it was to become the capital of the Kingdom of Italy, and the population for the first time exceeded 100,000, the size it had reached in 1300.

The major architectural influence during the late 13th and early 14th centuries was Arnolfo di Cambio, whose projects included the church of Santa Croce and the main body of Florence Cathedral, in the cheerful multi-colored marble of the north Italian style. He also designed the first part of the Palazzo della Signoria (or Palazzo Vecchio), the symbol of civic power in the city. After di Cambio's death, work was continued by the painter Giotto, who designed the Cathedral's bell tower. The Guilds, powerful trade and craft associations, had consolidated their power in the *Comune* by the end of the 13th century. During the next two centuries, responsibility for Florence's built environment shifted to merchants, artists and craftsmen, and professional people.

The birth of the Renaissance

The building of the distinctive dome over Florence Cathedral by Filippo Brunelleschi between 1420 and 1436 gave the city its enduring symbol. At 180 feet from floor to lantern and 140 feet in span, it was the first dome to rival the work of the Romans. In that sense, it inaugurated the Renaissance in Italy. At the same time, new ideas of urban design made Florence the workshop of early Renaissance

THE MEDICI

During the 15th and 16th centuries, Florence was the capital of the Renaissance, attracting poets, artists, architects, musicians, and scientists from Italy and throughout Europe to enjoy the patronage of the powerful banking families. These included such towering figures as Alberti, Botticelli, and Brunelleschi, followed by Leonardo da Vinci, Michelangelo, and Galileo.

For nearly 400 years, the Medici were associated with the patronage of the arts – not, as in most princely courts, aimed at a limited audience, but fully appreciated by the Florentine people. At this time,

Lorenzo the Magnificent, from a fresco (c.1634–6) by Giovanni Sangiovanni.

Florence was ruled by a Signoria, or city council, which was completely dominated by the Medici so that they ruled the city absolutely. Their influence outside Florence was equally powerful. Medici became popes and married into royal families.

The first of the great line, Giovanni di Bicci, born in 1360, financed the reconstruction of San Lorenzo. His son Cosimo inherited his love of buildings. He commissioned Michelozzo to reconstruct the San Marco convent, incorporating the first library open to the public.

The regime of the Signoria reached its climax with Lorenzo the Magnificent. At once a philosopher, classical scholar, statesman, and playboy, he encouraged great artists to work in Florence. Works of art in the Medici palace were eagerly displayed for foreign visitors to admire. Roman and Greek antiquities were discovered and studied systematically.

Not long after Lorenzo's premature

death in 1492 at the age of 43, his successor Pietro lo Sfortunato ("the Unfortunate") was driven out, and for a time Florence became a republic again. The Medici came back and ruled Florence from 1512 to 1527, when more uprisings restored the republic. Not long afterward, in 1532, Florence lost its independence as a city-state and became the capital of Tuscany. But the Medici were by no means finished. In 1540, Cosimo I moved into the Palazzo della Signoria and consolidated his power over the city. In 1569, he was awarded the title of Grand Duke. All his successors bore the title until the end of the Medici dynasty in 1743.

San Lorenzo, the first church of the Renaissance.

Cosimo de' Medici inherited a love of buildings from his father.

architecture and planning.

A street from the Cathedral to the Church of Santissima Annunziata became the site of one of the most important Renaissance schemes, involving architects over some 200 years. At the end of the vista from the Cathedral, extending to the northeast, was the piazza in front of the church. Here, on the eastern side, in 1427, Brunelleschi completed his Foundling Hospital, with its elegant arcade.

When Brunelleschi completed his Foundling Hospital, in 1427, with its elegant arcade, he began a design process that lasted for two centuries, with a variety of architects complementing his schemes around the square. This model of a unified urban space quickly spread to other cities.

Some 25 years later, a new entrance to the church from the square was designed by Michelozzo, with a central bay in harmony with Brunelleschi's arcade. In 1516, the architects Antonio da Sangallo the Elder and Baccio d'Agnolo were commissioned to design the building on the third side of the square, opposite Brunelleschi's Hospital. The architects decided to complement the style of the other two sides and provide a similar arcade. By 1600, the piazza was completed with the placing of two fountains and the equestrian statue of Grand Duke Ferdinand I on a central axis facing the street.

The provision of medieval urban space was usually related to a single building. In contrast, the piazza was the focus of a number of complementary buildings designed by a variety of architects. This model of a unified urban space quickly spread to other cities.

The Renaissance rebuilding of Florence created an extensive network of streets connecting major buildings and squares throughout most of the city. This grand scheme superimposed on an essentially medieval pattern introduced a new scale of planning, which was later used in Rome.

Florence was seen by contemporaries as exerting a wider influence. Around 1404, Leonardo Bruni, humanist and Chancellor of the Republic, described Florence as "in the center, like a grand master," with the walls containing the urban core. Beyond were the suburbs, estates, and towns under Florentine influence, stretching to the distant mountains. This image of Florence in its setting was close to the Renaissance concept of the ideal city.

The medallion by Andrea della Robbia is incorporated in Brunelleschi's Foundling Hospital.

This etching of c.1711 shows the Uffizi from the river, looking toward the Piazza della Signoria.

THE PONTE VECCHIO

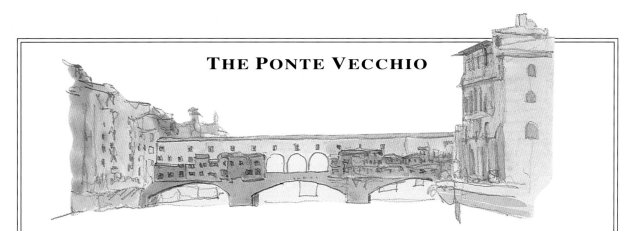

The Ponte Vecchio across the Arno River traces its origins to a wooden bridge built during Roman times. Later it was rebuilt in stone, but was destroyed in 1174.

The present bridge, some 300 feet long and 30 feet wide, was built during the 1340s. Early tenants of the 48 shops were the Guild of the Beccai (butchers and tanners), who used water from the river below. By 1495, the bridge was completely built up with small overhanging dwellings.

In the 1550s, the bridge was refurbished and incorporated into the Corridoio Vasariano for the First Duke of Tuscany, Cosimo de'Medici. This was a grand covered route linking the Palazzo Vecchio

Built in the 1340s, the Ponte Vecchio, with its overhanging buildings and elegant arches, is the only bridge to have survived the city's turbulent history.

to the Palazzo Pitti, and designed by Giorgio Vasari, who trained under Michelangelo. Vasari also designed the Uffizi, and he transformed the Ponte Vecchio itself, opening the center with three elegant arches on each side of the roadway. In 1593, the Grand Duke Ferdinando I evicted the Beccai for degrading the bridge with their trade and installed goldsmiths and jewelers, whose successors occupy the bridge to this day.

Of all Florence's bridges, the Ponte Vecchio is the only one to survive the city's turbulent history. All the other bridges were destroyed in World War II and were later rebuilt in their present form.

Beyond the Renaissance

After the death of the last of the Medici, Anna Maria Landovica, in 1743, the Grand Duchy fell under Austrian rule. After Italy became a national state in 1859, Florence was its first capital, from 1865 to 1871. Room had to be found for an entourage of some 50,000 people in a city of 100,000 inhabitants. There was a spate of house building. The outer walls were demolished, and a ring road was added.

During the 20th century, Florence acquired the usual ring of dreary suburbs. Under the fascists, by no means a bad time for Italian architecture, the world-renowned architect Pier Luigi Nervi designed the Berta sports stadium with its dramatic shell of reinforced concrete. Another addition was a rail station, tactfully constructed in the same materials and colors as the nearby church of Santa Maria Novella.

No major building was lost in World War II. More damage was done by the flood of 1966, and by a terrorist bomb which destroyed part of the Uffizi in 1993. But the city center retains its grandeur. Legislation prevents the erection of unsympathetic buildings, and cars have been banned from the central area. Amid the inevitable throngs of tourists, Florentines continue to use and enjoy their city.

BARCELONA

*The ancient Catalan city is famed for its modern buildings,
which can still startle the unprepared visitor.*

*Ceramic detail from
Gaudí's Parc Güell.*

Barcelona is the capital of Catalonia, a region of Spain with its own language, laws, and institutions. From a part of a powerful feudal system, it grew to embrace the Industrial Revolution, expanded hugely in the 19th century, and became one of the leading artistic centers of Europe in the 20th. This turmoil of change is reflected not only in the city's buildings, but in its very plan.

A Carthaginian city

The site of Barcelona, north of the mouth of the Llobregat River, has been inhabited since prehistoric times. The Carthaginians founded a city here in the 3rd century B.C. and named it after their leader Hamilcar Barca. In 146 B.C.,

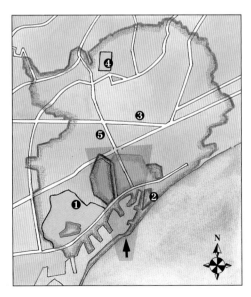

Catalonia became a Roman province, and the colony of Barcino was established in around 15 B.C. and encircled with a fortified wall with 78 towers.

The enclosed area of some 25 acres was laid out on the grid plan, with four gates at either end of the main north–south and east–west streets. At the highest point near the northern gate was the Temple of Augustus, of which a few columns still stand behind the medieval cathedral.

Barcino was both a fort and a symbol of Rome's authority. The surrounding territory, and its Roman citizens who cultivated the land, were governed throughout the high Imperial period by an administration which was accommodated within the original walls.

The *colonia* became part of the Visigothic Kingdom in the 5th century and was later absorbed into the Moorish empire. The Moors were driven out of Catalonia in the 10th century. The monastery of Santa Maria de Ripoll, the finest example of Romanesque architecture in Spain, dates from this time.

A capital city

During the Middle Ages, the Kingdom of Aragon and Catalonia dominated the Mediterranean world. As its capital city, Barcelona was extended by King Jaume I in the 13th

*This 14th-century
cathedral in the* Barri
Gòtic *replaced a
Romanesque
building.*

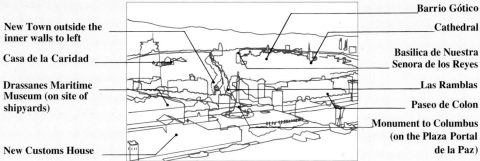

The reconstruction shows a view of the harbor and Barcelona's Old Town, c.1570.

New Town outside the inner walls to left

Casa de la Caridad

Drassanes Maritime Museum (on site of shipyards)

New Customs House

Barrio Gótico

Cathedral

Basilica de Nuestra Senora de los Reyes

Las Ramblas

Paseo de Colon

Monument to Columbus (on the Plaza Portal de la Paz)

*The Romanesque portal
of Santa Maria de Ripoll.*

century. He built an outer circle of walls enclosing an area ten times larger than the Roman city. The old city center, or *Barri Gòtic*, remained the administrative center.

Extensive building projects during the 14th century, interrupted only briefly by the Black Death of 1348, filled up the new area. King Pere III (1336–87) had the shipyards reconstructed; seven bays of the work survive. Also from this period date the Llotya or Stock Exchange – the oldest of its kind and still in use – and the Saló de Cent, seat of the city council.

In the late 15th century, Catalonia was absorbed into the Kingdom of Castile and Aragon. From 1697, the city was refortified against the War of Spanish Succession. On the losing side in 1714, Catalonia was occupied by the Bourbons, who built the Ciutadella or citadel, a military complex requiring the demolition of some 2,000 houses. In 1775, a new harbor district was built called La Barceloneta, which was regarded as one of the most enlightened examples of town planning in 18th-century Europe.

By the 18th century, Barcelona was dominated by aristocrats, and artisans belonged to guilds or trade associations. The social structure changed with the Industrial Revolution. Immigrants came to work in the new factories, whose owners built grandiose new houses along Las Ramblas, replanned as the city's finest street. One of the most elegant legacies of this time is the Plaça Reial, designed by Francese Daniel Molina in the 1830s, a spacious square off Las Ramblas.

Throughout the 19th century, Barcelona changed rapidly. The French occupied the city briefly during the Napoleonic wars. Factory workers rioted in protest against their cramped and squalid conditions.

In 1859, plans were put forward by the engineer and planner Ildefons Cerdà to accommodate the growing industrial population. The small medieval town was transformed into a modern metropolis stretching from the sea to the mountains. The "Eixample" (extension) was on a grid pattern divided by streets 65 feet wide. In contrast to Haussmann's rebuilding of Paris, Cerdà's work involved little demolition. Most of it was built on open country.

The focus of the plan was the Plaça de Catalunya, from which the impressive Passeig de Gràcia extended to the northwest. Two large diagonal avenues were planned through the Eixample. The rigid formality of the plan was offset by garden squares and parks, with buildings occupying only two sides of each

GAUDÍ

Antoní Gaudí Cornet (1852–1926) was a radically original Catalan architect. His flowing style placed him at the head of the Art Nouveau movement in Spain. In his Parc Güell housing project, Gaudí was influenced by the English idea of the garden city. He also designed numerous houses, such as Casa Batlló and Casa Mila, with flowing façades and windows fronted by tortuous iron balconies.

His undisputed masterpiece is the Church of the Sagrada Família (begun 1884) which culminates in a fantastic surreal design topped by four pierced conical towers. This extraordinary church has not always been popular. But today Gaudí's buildings are synonymous with Barcelona.

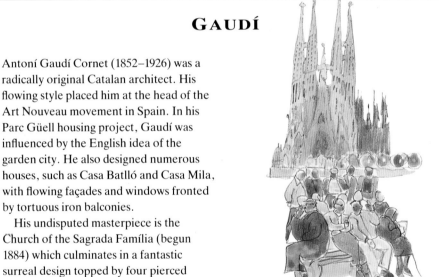

*La Sagrada Família
(the Holy Family)
survives as the*   *unfinished
monument to the
genius of Gaudí.*

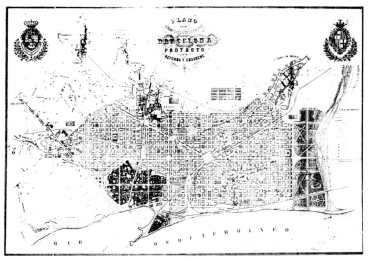

Cerdà's plans transformed Barcelona, their rigid formality diffused by diagonal avenues and garden squares with buildings on only two sides.

The least sign of Catalan nationalism, including the use of the language, was punished.

When Franco died in 1975, Barcelona sprang to life again. It is now emphatically the capital of Catalonia, not just another Spanish city. Street signs are in Catalan first and Spanish second. There is a huge collection of the works of Pablo Picasso, the province's most famous artist, occupying several of the medieval palaces. In 1992, Barcelona hosted the Olympic Games, at the same time holding a cultural festival. Rebuilding continues as fast as ever in this constantly changing city – much of it at the expense of the drab buildings put up during the Franco era, while Barcelona's Catalan heritage is proudly preserved.

block. However, landowners and developers were not prepared to sacrifice so much and soon built over these spaces.

The Universal Exhibition of 1888, which attracted more than 2 million visitors, was the stimulus to implement the plan to expand the city. The site of the exhibition was Ciutadella Park, an open space since the demolition of the citadel in 1868. The park was elegantly laid out by Josep Foutseré Mestres, assisted by the young Antoni Gaudí, who also designed the gates to the entrance.

In Barcelona, exhibitions have played an important and perhaps unique role in innovation. For example, the Grand Hotel International along the Passeig de Colom, near the waterfront, designed by Domènech i Montaner to house 2,000 visitors, was completed for the 1888 exhibition.

It became clear that Cerdà's plan for the Eixample was too uniform in layout. In 1903, Léon Jaussely, a French architect, won a competition with a scheme to divide the grid layout into zones. His plan, in modified form, was implemented in 1917. Amid considerable controversy, a large street, the Via Laietana, was driven from the Eixample through the medieval center to the port. The city also gained an underground rail system.

The International Exhibition of 1929 was conceived as a means of providing employment for some 40,000 workers at the depth of the world slump. It included two German pavilions by Mies van der Rohe, which had a profound influence on architecture worldwide.

Throughout the first part of the 20th century, Barcelona was one of the world's principal centers of art and architecture. In 1932, the radical Swiss architect Le Corbusier was invited to collaborate with local architects on a new plan for the city. This got as far as building a large apartment building, known as the Casa Block. But in 1936, the Spanish Civil War broke out.

Barcelona, firmly on the Republican side, was the last stronghold to surrender to Franco in 1939. After that, the city, and Catalonia as a whole, were heavily repressed by the victors.

Architecture merges with nature in the Park of Spanish Industry. These towers light up the man-made lake of St. George and the Dragon.

PRAGUE

Once the capital of the Holy Roman Empire, Prague has amassed a rich treasury of architecture; it is one of the world's most beautiful cities.

For centuries, Prague was not a city, but a collection of independent towns and villages straggling around two castles on opposite sides of a river. Despite decades of first Nazi, then Soviet domination, it retains a heterogeneous quality to this day, but at the same time its magnificent buildings are the envy of most European cities.

A town between two castles

The site of Prague is known to have been inhabited since Neolithic times. However, the present city has its origins late in the 9th century when Prague Castle (Pražskýhrad) was

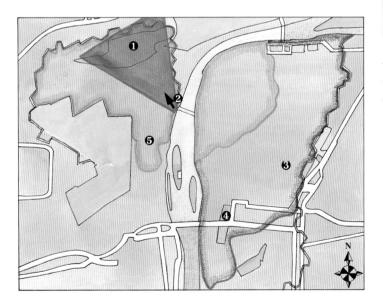

built beside a ford in the river Vltava, a little to the north of the center of Bohemia. This stronghold of the Czech tribe consisted of a long, narrow settlement with a fort for the leader and his entourage, and with accommodation for those serving the castle. Early in the 10th century, on the opposite bank of the river, 2½ miles south of Prague Castle, High Castle (Vyšhrad) was built on a 160-foot high hilltop.

In the early Middle Ages, Bohemia became part of the Holy Roman Empire and developed links with Western Europe. Prague became an important focus for trade, and in 973 gained the status of a bishopric.

Prague, today a unified city of ten administrative districts, was once a collection of autonomous towns coexisting side by side. They were built along both banks of the River Vltava, north of the center of Bohemia, on a suitable fording place.

The reconstruction shows the Lesser Town, Prague Castle and the new city walls built by Charles IV in the 1360s.

St Vitus's Cathedral _____

Vladislau Hall _____

Royal Palace _____

St Nicholas _____
(Lower Town)

Lobkowitz Palace
Chapel of All Saints

Lower Town Square
St Thomas's Church

Gate to Charles Bridge _____
Charles Bridge _____

Late in the 11th century, near the ford linking the two castles, the main marketplace was set up, today known as the Old Town Square (Stavoměstské náměsti). This square became the core of the Old Town (Staré Město), where foreign merchants enjoyed protection and used the Týn Court for trade. The square determined the surrounding irregular street layout. Around it a substantial town grew up, with palaces, convents and churches, large stone houses and humbler timber dwellings. Yet until it was granted a town charter, it could not be regarded as a city.

In 1231, King Wenceslas I (1230–53) started to enclose the Old Town with walls to the south and east (along the present Národni, Prikopy, and Revolicní streets). Later, the protection of the Old Town was extended with another wall on the bend of the river, also enclosing a space for mills, ironworks, and lumber yards.

About the same time, the surveyor and builder Eberhard began work on the new Gall Town (Havelské Město). It was based on a regular plan, with an elongated marketplace between the present Coal Market (Uhelmý trh) and the Fruit Market (Ovocný trh). At the center was the church of St. Gall (whose name in Czech is Havel) and the Royal Court of Law. The character of this part of town is still apparent from the arcades in Havelská Street, with cross vaulting on stone ribs; similar arcades once surrounded the market square.

Wenceslas' son, Přemysl Otakar II (1253–78), continued his father's work and founded the Lesser Town (Malá Strana) on the left bank of the river. This settlement was planned around a large rectangular marketplace and a new church of St. Nicholas. Surrounded by stone walls, Lesser Town was linked to Prague Castle, the Bishop's Court, and the Monastery of St. John with a stone bridge. Today, this town still

The Old Square, painted in 1866, dominated by the Týn Court and Gothic Church of 1365.

The spectacular vaulting of St. Vitus' Cathedral (right) was created by Peter Parler.

retains the layout of the square and several streets leading toward the Charles Bridge.

An extensive fire in 1291 destroyed many Romanesque timber structures. As a means of protecting the settlement from floods, the ground was artificially raised by about 10 feet to its present level, providing further opportunities to rebuild Prague in the Gothic style.

At the beginning of the 14th century, Prague consisted of small towns, each legally and administratively independent. The total area was probably about 300 acres, of which about 60 percent constituted the Old Town.

Capital of an empire

During the reign of the Emperor Charles IV (1346–78), Prague was transformed into the largest and most imposing city in central Europe. In 1348, Charles founded the University of Prague, and some seven years later, the city became the capital of the Holy Roman Empire. During the 1360s, he extended the Lesser Town toward the south and encircled it with a stone wall. He employed a French architect, Mathieu d'Arras, to build St. Vitus Cathedral. After the death of d'Arras, the talented architect Peter Parler of Gmünd, took over the building of the cathedral and many other fine structures, including the Charles Bridge which are some of the best examples of late Gothic architecture in Europe.

One of the major achievements of Charles' reign was the development of the New Town (Nové Město), adjoining the Old Town. Following the precedent of the Old Town, he specified rules to encourage rapid growth, including the building of structures within 18 months of land purchase, and the exemption

THE TOWNS OF PRAGUE

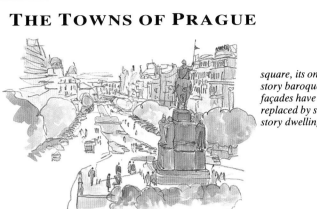

Wenceslas Square, dominated by the equestrian statue of St. Wenceslas, is the focus of the New Town. More akin to a wide boulevard than a conventional *square, its once two-story baroque façades have been replaced by seven-story dwellings.*

Modern Prague is a unified city, made up of ten districts. However, the characteristics of once autonomous towns remain to this day. Prague Castle, and its vicinity, Hradčany, reveal the very origins of Prague. Situated at the foot of the castle, Lesser Town is now separated from the rest of the city by large parklands and the River Vltava.

Along the river on the right bank is the Old Town, with its restored square. The layout of streets and squares (including the old Jewish quarter to the north) have remained since the Middle Ages; only the façades have changed in a progression of architectural styles.

The New Town of Charles IV with its massive Wenceslas Square – more akin to a wide boulevard, measuring 2,250 feet in length – was the gathering point of demonstrations in the "Velvet Revolution" of 1989. Dominating this space is the equestrian statue of St. Wenceslas.

ments, including some 100 ecclesiastical buildings and numerous markets, had a population of some 50,000 and covered an area of some 2,000 acres. Under Charles' son, Wenceslas IV, until 1400 when Prague ceased to be the capital of the Holy Roman Empire, building activity continued, but on a limited scale.

An over-powerful church (owning 50 percent of all agricultural land in the country) and its corrupt administration in Prague triggered the Hussite Revolution. In the conflicts that followed during 1419, the Lesser Town was virtually destroyed.

Prague under the Habsburgs

The Habsburg King Ferdinand I ascended to the throne of Bohemia in 1526. In 1534, Ferdinand extended Prague Castle and laid out the Royal Garden as the first Italianate garden north of the Alps. Nearby stands his Royal Summer House, a small belvedere which is the first Renaissance building in Prague.

Although many fine buildings were con-

Prague, c.1493, a series of self-contained towns separated by parklands and the River Vltava.

from taxes for new inhabitants for 12 years.

With its focus in Wenceslas Square, the New Town was enhanced by straight streets, with an imposing church and monastic buildings, many of which were either destroyed or drastically altered through the course of time. The streets were generously wide: Jecuá (Barley Street) spans some 89 feet. Charles Square covers an area of some 20 acres, making it the largest of its kind in Europe.

At the end of the 14th century, Prague, with its two castles and collection of town settle-

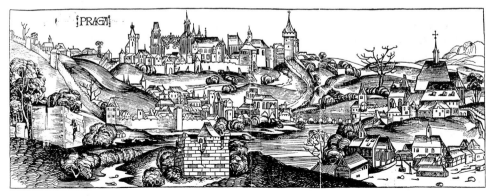

structed in the 16th century, the Renaissance in Prague had little influence on the medieval pattern of the city. The Gothic towers which determined the city's medieval character still soared over the façades of Renaissance palaces. Yet new architectural styles were being absorbed. The reign of Emperor Rudolph II (1584–1612) ushered in a period which became known as "Golden Prague." By the beginning of the 17th century, Prague had become the center of Mannerism, a style characterized by exaggerated scale and perspective.

Disputes between Catholics and Protestants continued, culminating in the Thirty Years' War. In the conflict, Bohemia lost some 25 percent of its population, who left in voluntary exile. During this time, Prague was virtually deserted and extensively looted. However, the city became an ideal location for the rising Catholic nobility. Many palaces and Jesuit colleges were erected in the new Baroque style. Between 1623 and 1630, the remarkable Váldštejinský Palace was built at the center of Lesser Town. It was separated from the rest of the town by a new square and an enclosed landscaped garden. The palace became a magnet for other residences and set the pattern for similar buildings.

During the Baroque period, Prague was transformed by construction on a new scale. Towering buildings with domes and curved walls changed the skyline. New palaces, town houses, monasteries, and churches were incorporated into the urban pattern. The city's appearance changed further when the Gothic walls and medieval towers were replaced by new fortifications.

The modern city

In 1817 Karlín, the first suburb, was built to the east of the Old Town, and became the

THE ROYAL WAY

The Old Town Bridge Tower is probably the finest Gothic gateway in central Europe. Built by Peter Parler c.1400, it was renovated by Josef Mocken in the 19th century.

The Royal Way was the processional route for the coronation ceremony of the Habsburgs. It was last used in 1836 for the Austrian Emperor Ferdinand V.

The procession began in the New Town and gathered at the end of Wenceslas Square (where the Horse Gate once stood). It moved across to Charles Square and along the Naprikope thoroughfare, leading to the Powder Tower, which formed a grand entrance to the Old Town. From here, the procession moved west along the now-pedestrianized Galetná leading to the Týn Church, facing the Old Town Square. Having performed the appropriate ceremonies at the entrance of this church, the procession passed toward the splendid Charles Bridge across the Vltava River, leading to the Lesser Town.

The route followed the broad Bridge Alley along the south side of St. Nicholas Church and the steep Nerudora Street. From here, it was a short distance to Hradčany Square and the castle, where the heir to the throne was presented to the people.

industrial area of the city. To the west of New Town, on the left bank of the river, another industrial district developed, called Smichor.

During the early part of the 19th century, through the influence of Romanticism, considerable green spaces were added, with gardens, tree-lined avenues and parks at the edge of the city. By the middle of the century, Prague's total population had reached 150,000.

The river embankments were developed, and a rail station was built. In the 1870s, the city walls were demolished, allowing Prague to expand. New bridges spanning the river Vltava unified the city.

On October 28, 1918, the Czechoslovak Republic was established, with Prague as the capital and seat of government. In the 1920s, Prague, now under a single city administration, had a population of some 670,000 and consisted of eight districts, 11 townships, and 26 villages. In the suburbs, space between buildings was widened with gardens and trees, contributing to the green appearance of the city.

After World War II, when Czechoslovakia came under communist rule, Prague was quickly expanded, with many housing projects, often badly sited and poorly constructed, accommodating as many as 15,000 people each. By 1974, the city incorporated more than 50 villages, accommodating 1 million inhabitants in all.

After the collapse of communism in 1989 and the subsequent division in 1992 between the Czech and Slovakia territories, Prague became the capital of the Czech Republic. The city now covers some 200 square miles, with 1.5 million inhabitants mostly living in an extensive peripheral urban development of drab apartment buildings with poor amenities.

Since 1971, the inner city of Prague has been a conservation area, and many imposing buildings are protected as national monuments. The historic center of Prague is now recognized as one of the most attractive cities in Europe. A pedestrian route has been created along the Royal Way, leading past the Powder Tower through the Old Town Square to Charles Bridge.

Yet outside the center, the urban environment of Prague has been sadly neglected and is now in urgent need of rehabilitation. Today Prague, with a history of more than 1,000 years, is trying to come to terms with the needs of a modern democratic state.

The view from Letna Hill offers a compound image of the bridges of Prague across the river Vltava which play a vital role in unifying the whole city.

THE PRAGUE DEFENESTRATIONS

Early in the 15th century, a tradition began in Prague known as defenestration: those who incurred the wrath of the people were thrown out of upper windows.

In 1419, Hussites stormed the New Town Hall and threw out of the windows ten citizens, including three eminent consuls. This led to the Hussite revolution, with major consequences for Prague. Another defenestration occurred in 1483, when people stormed the Town Hall and threw the Mayor of the New Town out of a second-story window. King Vladislav was forced to move to Prague Castle, where he built the magnificent Vladislav Hall, designed by the architect Benedikt Ried, the first wing added to a palace in Prague in the Renaissance style.

In 1618, three Catholic councillors were thrown from a castle window into the moat by angry Protestants. This confrontation between Protestants and Catholics was a forerunner of the bloody Thirty Years' War which convulsed Europe.

Religious reformer Jan Hus, who was burned at the stake in *1415, shown in a contemporary drawing.*

AMSTERDAM

*At one of the commercial and cultural centers of Europe,
Amsterdam effortlessly combines bourgeois respectability
with youthful radicalism.*

Amsterdam is a compact city of some 650,000 inhabitants. Its typically Dutch spick-and-span neatness contrasts with its status as the capital of European counterculture, with its relaxed atmosphere – and cafés openly selling soft drugs – attracting large numbers of youthful visitors year-round.

The dam on the Amstel

A fishing village was founded at the mouth of the river Amstel around 1200. The site on the shore of the inland Zuider Zee was protected from storms, but communicated with the North Sea. It soon became a thriving port. Around 1270, the inhabitants built a dam to control tidal surges, giving the settlement its name. In 1275, the Count of Holland granted "Amestelledamme" exemption from tolls on Dutch waterways. It was formally chartered as a city shortly before the Count annexed it in 1317.

Amsterdam was a stop for ships of the rising Hanseatic League sailing to Bruges. A trade grew up in grain, salt fish, beer, wine, lumber, and cloth, often carried in Dutch ships which undercut the rates of the Hanseatic traders.

The city needed to expand on a marshy site. The Dutch were masters of land reclamation, making enclosed areas known as polders protected from the sea by dykes, and gradually drained by wind power. The city was defended on its landward sides by walls and a moat. Around 1380 it was extended; a new moat was dug and a new wall built. The old moat became a canal inside the walls. This process was repeated several times, twice in the 15th century and three times shortly before 1600.

KEY

Extent at 1400
Extent at 1500
Extent in 1640
Extent at 1800
Reconstruction area

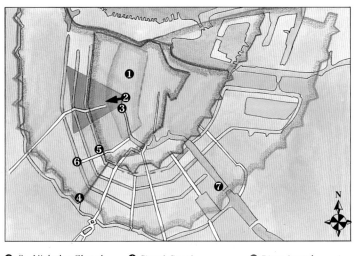

❶ St. Nicholas Church
❷ Dam Square
❸ City Hall
❹ Singel Canal
❺ Herengracht
❻ Prinsengracht
❼ River Amstel

0   K m   ½
0   Mi   ¼

The grandiose Trip House was built in 1662. Note the chimneys in the shape of mortars: the Trip family manufactured armaments. They moved from Liège to escape persecution. Jakob Trip had his and his wife's portraits painted by Rembrandt.

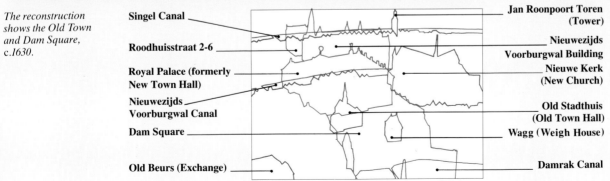

The reconstruction shows the Old Town and Dam Square, c.1630.

Singel Canal

Roodhuisstraat 2-6

Royal Palace (formerly New Town Hall)

Nieuwezijds Voorburgwal Canal

Dam Square

Old Beurs (Exchange)

Jan Roonpoort Toren (Tower)

Nieuwezijds Voorburgwal Building

Nieuwe Kerk (New Church)

Old Stadthuis (Old Town Hall)

Wagg (Weigh House)

Damrak Canal

Amsterdam soon outgrew its church of St. Nicholas, or the Oude Kerk, dating from around 1300. Soon after 1400, St. Catherine's, or the Nieuwe Kerk, was begun on the other side of the river near the original dam. The surrounding area became the Dam Square, the site of the City Hall and the city's principal square.

The Netherlands was part of the Holy Roman Empire, under the rule of the Habsburgs. The 16th century brought Protestantism. Radical Anabaptists occupied the City Hall; Puritans smashed the religious images in the Oude Kerk. In 1567, King Philip II of Spain sent the Duke of Alva to restore Catholicism. Amsterdam favored the Catholics, while the surrounding area was Protestant under William of Orange. The city was forced to yield in 1578. However, the new Protestant rule proved an unexpected blessing.

The Golden Age

In 1597, Cornelis Houtman's ships returned to Amsterdam from a two-year trading voyage to the East Indies, showing that such an expedition was feasible. In 1602, the Dutch East Indies Company was founded. An enormously lucrative trade, and the beginning of an empire, ensued. A West Indies Company followed in 1621; its members later founded New York.

Amsterdam rose as its rival, Antwerp, taken by the Spanish in 1585, declined. Protestant refugees flocked in from the occupied provinces. The city's religious tolerance also attracted expelled Portuguese Jews, who made Amsterdam a center of the gem trade.

Among many other consumer goods, the prosperous burghers wanted paintings. Artists crowded in to satisfy the demand: one such was Rembrandt van Rijn, who moved from Leiden in 1631.

THE AMSTERDAM HOUSE

Medieval Amsterdam was built of wood. After two fires in 1421 and 1453,

regulations enforced the use of brick. Land, often reclaimed from marsh, was expensive. This led to the typically tall, narrow Amsterdam house.

Deep piles were driven to build a house. Joists supporting the floor rested on side, load-bearing walls, while the front and back façades remained self-supporting, allowing large windows and providing light to deep rooms. A prominent feature was the stepped gable, known as a halsgevel, often with a lift for hoisting furniture and goods. Inside, staircases were narrow. Rooms were larger at the front and smaller at the back. This unpretentious style helped create a unified urban composition.

A frank late self-portrait by Rembrandt, who made and lost a fortune in the city's 17th century Golden Age.

At this time, the city center was replanned. Many of the splendid houses built by rich merchants at this time may still be seen. In 1655, a magnificent new City Hall was opened in Dam Square. The population was over 200,000.

A series of misfortunes

The second half of the 17th century brought the Netherlands war with England, an abortive French invasion, and the protracted War of Spanish Succession. The fighting sapped Amsterdam's wealth, and the city went into gradual decline. In the 1780s, civil disputes allowed the French to invade successfully, setting up the puppet Batavian Republic. In 1806, Napoleon's brother Louis was declared King of the Netherlands and took up residence in the City Hall, renamed the Royal Palace.

In 1813, the Netherlands gained its independence, but the revival of colonial trade failed to restore Amsterdam's prosperity. New, larger merchant ships could no longer navigate the shallow Zuider Zee, and trade moved to Rotterdam at the mouth of the Rhine.

The Netherlands was in recession during the mid-century, increasing Amsterdam's population as destitute people came in from the countryside. Overcrowding brought epidemics: 2,000 died of cholera in 1848–9. But the picture was not entirely gloomy. After 1848, the marshes around the city were drained, providing agricultural land and road and rail links. Industry revived and new suburbs were built.

A resilient city

Between 1870 and 1900, Amsterdam's population rose from 255,000 to 511,000. The Netherlands remained neutral in World War I, and in 1917, the Plan Zuid (south) added a spacious suburb in the best contemporary style. In 1935, an ambitious General Extension Plan was approved, including a ring of garden suburbs.

By this time, all of Europe was in a slump, and little was built. In 1940, the Germans invaded. There were then 80,000 Jews in the city. By the end of the war, fewer than 14,000 were left. The diary of Anne Frank, a young Jewish girl who hid in an attic until she was discovered and deported to die in a camp, vividly describes the horror of those times.

The new suburbs of the early 20th century were built in a modern but approachable style, with imaginative details such as this massive wooden doorway.

After the war, the Amsterdammers resumed the Extension Plan, building suburbs on reclaimed polders. As a seaport, the city never overtook Rotterdam. But Schiphol Airport became one of the busiest in Europe and made Amsterdam a center of communications.

So began an era of prosperity which has even weathered the recession of the 1990s – but not without reaction. From the mid-1960s, the radical Provos began a series of imaginative protests against the consumer society, including white-painted bicycles for everyone's free use to reduce motor traffic in the city. Although the Provos are gone, something of their idealism survives. Amsterdam is a good place to be young.

A bird's-eye view of the Jordan district, just outside the western curve of the

Prinsengracht, shows Amsterdam's typically tall, narrow houses with large windows.

MEXICO CITY

Bloodily founded on a place of human sacrifice, torn by earthquakes, choked with pollution and subsiding, this remains one of the world's great cities.

The stone Aztec Calendar, with the sun god at the centre.

KEY

▢ *Extent of the ancient Aztec city*

▢ *Extent at the beginning of the 20th century*

▢ *Reconstruction area*

❶ *Zócalo*
❷ *Chapultepec Castle*
❸ *National Palace*
❹ *Alameda*

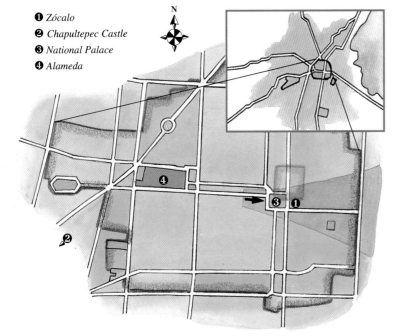

Built at an exhausting altitude on a sinking lake bed in a seismic zone, Mexico City could hardly claim to have an ideal site. It is also probably the most polluted city in the world, on most days shrouded in a lung-rotting brown haze. Yet this does not deter its inhabitants. Already the third largest city in the world, it is expected to overhaul São Paulo and Bombay in the next few years to become the biggest of all. Founded in 1522 on the site of the Aztec capital Tenochtitlán, it is one of the oldest cities in the New World, graced by a magnificent baroque cathedral sunk weirdly to the middle of its columns in the ground as its vast weight presses into the spongy soil.

The Mexican Megalopolis

The Aztecs were the last Nahuatl tribe to reach the central plateau of Mexico early in the 14th century. The name Mexico may have derived from Mexi, Mexitli, or Mecitli, all variations of Huitzilopochtli, the sun god of the Aztecs; or perhaps from Meztli, the moon god.

They founded their capital on a plateau 7,400 feet above sea level, surrounded by mountains and two snow-capped volcanoes. It was named Tenochtitlán, after their leader Tenoch. The present site of Zócalo, or Constitution Square, in today's Mexico City, was the original city center. Remains of some of the buildings can still be seen just north of the present National Palace adjoining the Cathedral.

The great Aztec Calendar Stone was found close to this site. This extraordinary astronomical chart is a sculpted stone 12 feet in diameter, with the sun god displayed in the center surrounded by the five ages of the uni-

The great Baroque cathedral, the largest in the Americas, was built by Cortés on the ruins of the Aztec palace. Although begun in 1567, it took some 250 years to complete.

The reconstruction shows the busy Zócalo, or market place, and the royal palace, c.1700.

Metropolitan Cathedral

National Palace

Zócalo

Monte de Piedad National Pawnshop

Il Profesa Church

Avenida Madero

Pitched market

City Hall (also known as Ayuntamiento)

Covered permanent market

verse. On the periphery of the stone are 22 hieroglyphics marking stages in the complex calendar, which combined a sacred period of 260 days with a 365-day year.

At that time, the area around the present cathedral was an island in the middle of a lake called Texcoco, 160 acres in extent, somewhat larger than Vatican City in Rome. The Aztecs extended this main island with floating islands called *chinampas,* made from huge wicker baskets filled with soil. They must have resembled the colorful "floating gardens" that today glide along the waterways of Xochimilco, south of Mexico City. The artificial islands eventually became rooted to the shallow lake bottom, forming groups separated by canals. The Aztecs planted them with maize, added trees, and later built huts.

The islands were linked to the shore by broad earthen causeways converging on the middle of the city. There was a dike 10 miles long to prevent flooding and protect the reclaimed land. As the ground stabilized, the Aztecs, like the Venetians, built houses on foundations of wooden piles, using the canals for transportation inside the city. Also like the Venetians, they extended their control to the surrounding lands. Under Montezuma I (1440–68), Tenochtitlán, with a population of as much as 200,000, became the capital of an extensive empire.

In the central square, the Aztecs built a great pyramid with many temples, other pyramids for lesser gods, palaces for chiefs, and groups of houses for priests. Another important complex was Tlaltelolco, with a splendid temple to the god of war, Huitzilopochtli. There were schools for the *mestizo,* or priesthood, as well as for dancing, poetry, and singing. The city was divided into 20 wards, each with its own tribal government.

Life on earth for the Aztecs was directly linked to the power of the sun. If the sun should vanish from the heavens, life for the Aztecs would end forever. To guarantee the sun's continued existence, they offered their god sacrifices, particularly human hearts, which they cut from the living bodies of the sacrificial victims and laid in carved troughs. The Aztecs waged war continuously, taking prisoners in large numbers to provide a regular supply of

human beings for sacrifice.

Although the Aztecs built magnificent structures and worked out highly accurate calendars, they apparently failed to discover the wheel. Any goods which could not be transported by canal were carried by bearers on platforms. There were no horses; these were yet to come from the Old World.

The Aztecs believed that a bearded white man would come from the east to claim their kingdom as his own. When the Spanish arrived early in the 16th century, the Aztec ruler Moctezuma II took their leader Hernando Cortés to be this god. He urged his people not to oppose Cortés. The Spanish had other ideas and killed Moctezuma. His successor Cuauhtémoc, the last Aztec leader, fought on against the *conquistadores,* but within two years the Spaniards had conquered the mighty Aztec empire. Cortés reduced the city to rubble.

The Alameda (left) once a swampy area known as "the burning place" where victims of the Spanish Inquisition met their deaths, became the first city park complete with Italian statues and water fountains.

This contemporary wall painting (top) shows the Aztecs greeting Cortés as a god.

A CRUEL PLACE

The present National Palace in Zócalo, planned exclusively for Spaniards, was built on an earlier Aztec site.

Zócalo, the central square, has witnessed awesome events: human sacrifices offered to Aztec gods, the slaughter of Aztecs by *conquistadores,* the burning of heretics by the Inquisition. Many of its present buildings date from the time of Cortés, incorporating stone taken from demolished Aztec structures. The Cathedral, begun in 1567, took 250 years to complete and is the largest in the Americas. Its adjoining sanctuary, the Sagrario Metropolitano, is heavily sculptured in the Mexican baroque style, locally named *Churrigueresque.* The National Palace, much altered since the time of Cortés, was built on the site of an earlier Aztec palace.

For 300 years after the arrival of the *conquistadores,* Mexico was ruled by Spain. The territory of New Spain, stretching from California to Panama, was rich in gold and silver. Mexico City, the new capital constructed from the ruins of Tenochtitlán in magnificent style, was referred to as "The City of Palaces." At the time when the Dutch were setting up an outpost at the tip of Manhattan Island, Mexico City was a city of 60,000 households.

A succession of Spanish viceroys, often cruel and corrupt, ruled over Mexico. Under their oppression, priests became the instrument of revolution, rebelling from 1810 until Spain granted Mexico its independence in 1821.

The first president of Mexico was a Zapotec Indian, Benito Juárez. In 1857 he implemented sweeping reforms, not the least of which was the separation of Church and State. Opponents of his reforms invited Maximilian, Archduke of Austria, to form a Mexican Empire, backed by the Church and the ambitious Napoleon III of France, who nursed a passion for acquiring colonial territory.

A comic opera unfolded in Mexico City when a naive Maximilian and his pampered wife Carlotta arrived on June 12, 1864, complete with French troops, to install themselves in the 18th-century Chapultepec Castle (on a site once known to the Aztecs as "the hill of the grasshoppers"). Here, for the next three years of their short reign, they led a life of ostentation and indulgence. The Emperor's chief public act was to lay out the Paseo de la Reforma, stretching north-east from his castle.

When France withdrew its support, the Emperor was quickly brought before a firing squad. His wife went mad, but lived on until 1927. Their splendid castle is now a museum. Mexico was a republic again.

With intermittent revolutions and 35 presidents in the next 53 years, Mexico was a troubled place until peace was established in 1920. Yet even taking this time into account, of all Latin American countries, Mexico has probably enjoyed the greatest political stability.

Paseo de la Reforma, modeled on the Champs-Elysées, was laid out by Emperor Maximilian in 1865. The Angel Monument in the foreground was erected in 1910 to celebrate 100 years of independence.

PARIS

*The most elegant expression of 19th-century city planning
was as much the result of concern for the maintenance of
public order as for urban beauty.*

KEY

▢ *Extent at 1180*

▢ *Extent in the reign of
Charles V, 14th
century*

▢ *Extent at 1676*

▢ *Extent at the time of
the Revolution*

▢ *Extent in mid-19th
century*

▢ *Reconstruction area*

❶ *Louvre*
❷ *Notre Dame*
❸ *Hôtel de Ville*
❹ *Place Royale (now
Place des Vosges)*

❺ *La Défense*
❻ *Place Louis XV (now
Place de la Concorde)*

❼ *Eiffel Tower*
❽ *Champs Elysées*
❾ *River Seine*

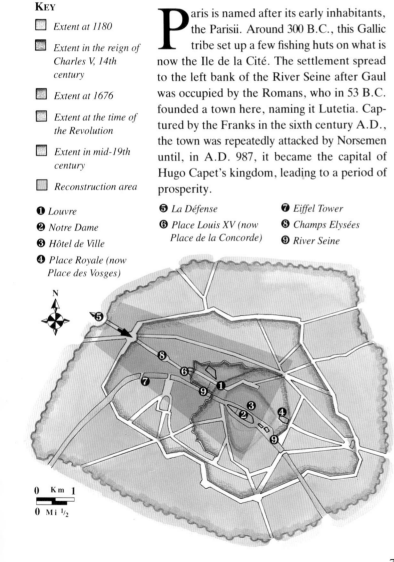

Paris is named after its early inhabitants, the Parisii. Around 300 B.C., this Gallic tribe set up a few fishing huts on what is now the Ile de la Cité. The settlement spread to the left bank of the River Seine after Gaul was occupied by the Romans, who in 53 B.C. founded a town here, naming it Lutetia. Captured by the Franks in the sixth century A.D., the town was repeatedly attacked by Norsemen until, in A.D. 987, it became the capital of Hugo Capet's kingdom, leading to a period of prosperity.

The Seine was narrow enough to be controlled by towers on each side. The city walls ran along both sides of the river, allowing Paris to develop freely within the fortified enclosure.

During the 12th and 13th centuries, Paris grew rapidly. The Louvre Palace was built, originally as a fortress, and the Cathedral of Notre Dame and the university were founded. However, the regular street pattern of the Roman town was lost, and Paris became a medieval city of narrow and winding streets. There were no large public urban spaces, although there were many private gardens and much open ground away from the city center,

This striking view of Notre Dame Cathedral (1163–1235) from the southeast shows the impressive slender flying buttresses which, with gabled transepts and delicate flèche, rise some 300 feet above ground in the heart of Paris.

The reconstruction shows the view looking down the Champs-Elysées towards the Louvre Palace, c.1740.

Place Vendôme

Church of La Madeleine

Place de la Concorde

Arc de Triomphe

Avenue des
Champs-Elysées

Palais du Louvre

Pont Royal

River Seine

Grand Palais

Jardin des Tuileries

so that Paris was still semi-rural in appearance. During the Renaissance, as the city expanded, the open land was progressively built over.

The age of grandeur

Between the 16th and 18th centuries, there was considerable development in some of the outer parts of the city, though little rebuilding in the medieval core. However, the Champs-Elysées was established, extending to the west of the city. During this period also, five major squares were built as settings for statues of kings: the Place Dauphine, Place Royale (now called Place des Vosges), Place des Victoires, Place Vendôme, and what is now the Place de la Concorde. Tree-lined *grands boulevards*

replaced the walls when Louis XIV tore them down and replaced them with fortifications suited to modern defensive needs and farther outside the city.

In the 16th century, the Louvre was rebuilt, and the Tuileries Gardens and the Hôtel de Ville were constructed. During the 17th and 18th centuries, the city grew in size and amenities: the Ile de Saint-Louis was developed and became a desirable residential quarter with a character that it still possesses today.

Cultural life flourished until Louis XIV, feeling restricted by the confines of the narrow streets, moved to Versailles. After the Revolution, Napoleon Bonaparte made strong efforts, from 1798 on, when he declared he

would make Paris the most beautiful city in the world. He built bridges, opened new thoroughfares, and raised monuments in honor of his victories. However, the transformation of Paris on a grand scale was finally achieved under Napoleon III during the 1850s, inspired in part by his years in England.

The transformation of Paris

Georges-Eugène Haussmann took full control of the transformation of Paris in the 1850s, a task for which he was made a baron. As Prefet de la Seine, he was the chief administrator of the capital and had a seat in the national government. He was answerable only to

---

THE SIGNIFICANCE OF VERSAILLES

The palace of Versailles was begun in 1668 by the architect Louis Le Vau and the park designer André Le Nôtre for Louis XIV. Its site was about a quarter of the current size of Paris, with paths radiating out from circular clearings. The palace was linked directly with Paris and the Louvre in a decisive and monumental manner with a broad ceremonial way across the countryside, disappearing over the horizon to link with the Champs-Elysées in Paris itself. To this day, the imposing thoroughfare provides a major exit from the capital.

The planning principles used in Versailles had an important influence on the design of cities that followed. It was the first time that such a large urban complex,

Versailles in its royal splendor was designed as a formal building xomplex of immense proportions. Set in an extravagant geometric layout, it inspired numerous city planning developments.

a building more than 2,000 feet long – was placed in direct contrast with nature, visually dominating limitless space and greenery. Of equal significance were the diagonal paths and focal points in the landscape, forming an expression of immense power and grandeur. The stately

geometry of Versailles and its grand scale later inspired such extravagant city planning developments as Karlsruhe in Germany (1720); Washington D.C. (1790); and even in the 20th century, New Delhi in India (1912) and Canberra in Australia (1925).

Expansive radiating boulevards, tree-lined along regular building façades, were the hallmark of Haussmann's transformation of Paris. Renowned landmarks such as the Eiffel Tower dominate the almost uniform skyline.

THE FIRST MAJOR SQUARE

The Place Royale (now Place des Vosges), laid out close to the Bastille in 1612, was the first major square in Paris. It became the prototype of residential squares which were virtually separated from through traffic. The central space with an equestrian statue of Louis XIII was surrounded with buildings of uniform design. An arcaded ground floor provided sheltered access and interconnected the houses. It also concealed store-fronts, which would have detracted from the dignity of the unified façades.

The Place Royale is of great significance to the history of European urban design and is the prototype for the integrated residential square. As a fashionable meeting place where tournaments were staged, Place Royale in its time became the focus of all Paris until the city began to grow westward.

Napoleon III. Urban design, particularly in existing cities, seems most successful when powerful political will is combined with ruthless vision. Haussmann was said to have "a backbone of iron." Without his inexorable determination, this transformation would never have taken place.

Although Paris was the first city to be replanned on such a scale, the inspiration may have come from London, where Napoleon III lived between 1838 and 1840. Here, he would have seen the sumptuous new Regent Street and the extensive parks nearby.

Haussmann created a new urban form essentially by placing a ruler on a city map, making straight lines through the crowded, narrow streets of medieval Paris. He demolished everything that stood in the way: 43 percent of all houses in the city were torn down to make way for the boulevards, many of which were as much as 400 feet wide.

These huge public works were carried out in a manner that would have pleased the highest treasury official in any government today. Public expenditure was seen as an investment which could be recovered from rising taxes and property prices, and so in the end would pay for itself. In the 17 years that Haussmann worked on the project, he was reputed to have spent 2.5 billion francs.

The state expropriated the land with money borrowed from building contractors, who also agreed to demolish old houses, erect new ones, and build the boulevards lined with rows of trees. The contractors agreed to hand the properties over to the state when the work was finished. Rents for the new buildings were high to cover the interest on the land. The boulevards provided new traffic arteries, effectively cleared slums, and provided work for the unemployed. They had another, less benign significance. Built in the aftermath of the unrest of 1848, which had culminated in large-scale riots in 1852, the wide, straight streets gave easy access to troops and artillery and made it possible to clear the areas around large public buildings.

The poor, although considerable in numbers, lacked the unity to mount an effective protest against the redevelopment and therefore suffered swift eviction. In contrast, investors and leaseholders were well compensated.

Contractors were required to build façades according to Haussmann's requirements, but what lay behind them was left to speculative builders, who adopted the fastest construction for the largest profit. To this day, much of the space between the boulevards remains of uneven quality.

Grandeur and gaiety

Although not popular at the time, the planning achievements in Paris are today regarded as extraordinary. They include the eastern extension of the Rue de Rivoli; the radiating roads around the Place de l'Etoile; and the Avenue de l'Opèra, which many regard as Haussmann's principal monument. Public parks were created which, unlike the London parks, were provided with restaurants, cafés, and even a racecourse for the entertainment of the Parisians. New rail stations, hospitals, colleges, and a glittering new opera house were added, as well as extensive market halls in cast iron at Les Halles. At the same time, public services of all kinds were improved.

Today Paris conveys a sense of place which is unique in the world. The great boulevards leading to splendid monuments and spacious parks epitomize the French love of elegance. It is also impossible to regard significant buildings in Paris without being aware of the process of urban design. Stand back to admire one monument, and you are immediately aware of a visual link with another.

The glass pyramid in the center of the Cour was designed by the American I. M. Pei.

Eiffel's Universal Exposition of 1867 (top) displayed the extent of contemporary innovation in art and industry.

Georges-Eugène Haussmann (above), as Seine Prefect, took control of the transformation of Paris in the 1850s.

Planning on a city-wide basis is still exemplified in Paris by new, bold architectural commissions and meticulous conservation schemes. Since the early 1970s, the French have been busy building a commercial center away from the heart of Paris, to the west at La Défense. The historic city is being both restored and embellished with modern buildings. Both projects are part of the planning tradition established in Paris three centuries before.

The Eiffel Tower was built for the Great Exhibition of 1889 by the engineer Gustave Eiffel. It was then the world's tallest structure at 984 feet.

Controversial when built on its site beside the Seine, it soon became the city's most famous landmark and the universally known symbol of Paris.

CHAMPS-ELYSEES

The Champs-Elysées, named after the classical paradise of the Elysian Fields, was first laid out around 1670 as the eastern end of Louis XIV's great processional route between the Louvre and Versailles. Through the centuries, it has been continuously developed and extended by successive governments into one of the world's grandest thoroughfares. From the 1830s on, it was the place where all Parisians with any claim to chic and sophistication had to be seen. The vista from the Tuileries, looking across the Place de la Concorde up the gentle slope for 1¾ miles to the Arc de Triomphe, remains truly imposing. Beyond the Arc, the line is continued along the Avenue de la Grande-Armée (named after Napoleon's army) to the Bois de Boulogne and the Pont de Neuilly.

Today this route extends farther to the new Paris and the La Défense arch, actually a cubical office block 360 feet high, with a hole in it, designed by Johann-Otto von Spreckelsen. The strong axis of this part of Paris is now reinforced by the construction of the glass pyramid at the Louvre on the east, designed by the American architect I. M. Pei. The Champs-Elysées, therefore, represents more than 300 years of continuity in design.

The neoclassical Arc de Triomphe, designed by J. F. Chalgrin in 1806, stands as the focus of 12 radiating avenues.

The arch, seen in the distance at the new commercial center at La Défense (below), is built on an axis with the Arc de Triomphe along the Champs-Elysées.

LONDON

The first of the giant cities, London remains a place where it is possible to enjoy life.

A Roman city built at a crossing place on the River Thames, London developed and prospered. Destroyed more than once, it nevertheless grew into the first city to have a population of more than two million, and the center of the largest empire the world has ever seen. Now, overtaken in size and frenzy by many a megalopolis in other parts of the world, London remains a civilized and moderate place, with spacious parks, green squares, and fine streets with dignified façades. Outside the ancient City, the central area retains some of the character of the original villages which were engulfed as London expanded. Beyond these, miles of suburbs stretch away into the countryside.

The fort on the lake

London began as a small Celtic village on the northern bank of the Thames, probably near the present site of the Tower. Its name may derive from the Celtic *Ilyn-din,* "the fort on the lake." No buildings survive from this period, but Celtic remains have been discovered in the river upstream near today's Battersea Bridge, including weapons and hundreds of skulls, carefully preserved according to Celtic funeral ritual.

The city of Londinium is a Roman creation. When the Romans invaded Britain in A.D. 43, they chose the site because the tidal river was suitable for their fleet, and there was a convenient place to build a bridge for the army. Seventeen years later, the vengeful Queen Boadicea attacked and burned the Roman city. But the Romans soon rebuilt it, and by A.D. 100, it had become the trading capital of Britain, with quays and warehouses and a permanent wooden bridge.

By the middle of the 3rd century, Londinium had roughly the same extent as the present

Parts of Londinium's wall, which encircled the Roman city survive to this day.

KEY

☐ *Extent of Roman Londinium*

▨ *Extent in 1660*

▨ *Extent in 1820*

☐ *Reconstruction area*

❶ *Tower of London*
❷ *Westminster Abbey*
❸ *St. Paul's Cathedral*
❹ *Buckingham Palace*

❺ *Regent's Park*
❻ *Tower Bridge*
❼ *Canary Wharf*
❽ *Oxford Street*

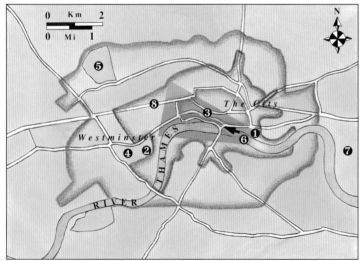

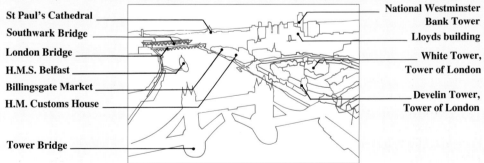

The reconstruction shows a view along the Thames of the City of London and Southwark from Tower Bridge, c.1750.

St Paul's Cathedral

Southwark Bridge

London Bridge

H.M.S. Belfast

Billingsgate Market

H.M. Customs House

Tower Bridge

National Westminster Bank Tower

Lloyds building

White Tower, Tower of London

Develin Tower, Tower of London

City of London, with perhaps 50,000 inhabitants. The city occupied a semicircular area of about 320 acres to the north of the Thames, the river forming the straight side. It was surrounded by a wall almost 3 miles long, over 20 feet high, and 8 feet thick. At a later date, the walls were strengthened with bastions, towers, and a fort.

Inside the walls, the main streets were paved. The workers lived in small, low huts or wooden houses, with thatched or shingle roofs, the Roman elite in substantial dwellings grouped around courtyards with fountains.

In 288, Londinium's importance was recognized by Rome, and it was given the proud name of Augusta. It was the largest city in Britain and the fifth largest in the western part of the Empire.

In 410, threatened by Germanic forces from its northern borders, Rome recalled its troops from Britain, and Londinium began to crumble. In 851, the Danes sacked it and destroyed much of what was left of the Roman city. Yet the spirit of the people survived, and rebuilding soon began under Alfred, King of Wessex.

The two cities

Londontown, as it was then called by its citizens, expanded northward. South of London Bridge, the settlement of Southwark also grew and became a royal borough, with rights to hold a market fair.

After his accession in 1042, King Edward the Confessor moved to a new palace 1½ miles upstream at Westminster, then on an island surrounded by marshes. The division of royal and mercantile power had a profound effect on the future development of London, which was reinforced when in 1066 William, Duke of Normandy, was crowned king in Westminster. After that event, Westminster was associated

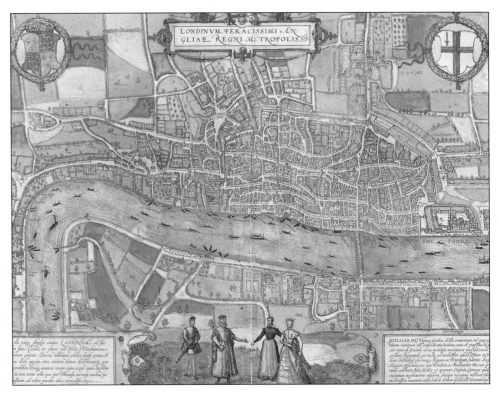

with the monarchy and the administration of the kingdom.

The rich and powerful City of London secured special privileges from the king. The first mayor was elected in 1192, a new St. Paul's Cathedral was started, and the White Tower (the central keep of the Tower of London) was completed in 1097. At Westminster in the same year, King William II built Westminster Hall, the largest building of its kind in Europe. The nobles at the court had fine riverside houses with gardens sloping down to the waterside. In 1197, the City started work on a new London Bridge, this time in stone.

Within the City's Roman walls, pierced with six gates, there were religious houses and

This plan of c.1580 shows the city growing beyond the walls. The population, including surrounding hamlets and villages, was 200,000.

merchant mansions, small burial grounds, and courtyards. At the end of the 12th century, some 40,000 people lived in this confined area and worshiped in more than 100 churches.

In the 14th century, London outside the walls began to grow rapidly, and the population had reached 200,000 by the year 1600. To control further growth, proclamations were issued prohibiting the building of new houses where none were built before within 3 miles of any City gate. The effect was to force more poor people into the existing overcrowded tenements and cottages.

Bubonic plague, which had ravaged Europe in the late 1340s, killing at least a third of the population of Britain, had remained endemic in overcrowded cities such as London. A serious outbreak in 1665 killed 100,000 in the city and spread to the rest of the country. The following year, a huge fire destroyed most of the largely wood-built city and much of St. Paul's Cathedral. The flames destroyed an area of 395 acres with 1,300 houses. Some 250,000 people were made homeless.

Reborn from the flames

Sir Christopher Wren quickly produced new plans for London, on a grid pattern, diversified with focal points connected by radiating avenues. But this plan was too radical for Londoners, who after the devastation needed shelter more than fanciful plans for an ideal

The Great Fire destroyed some 1,300 houses and many other fine wooden buildings.

A leather fire bucket – useless against the flames.

THE GREEN CITY

Bedford Square, started in 1776, with its central garden of grass and plane trees, was the first of the grand London squares. It combined dignified façades with a semi-formal landscape, and is little changed to this day.

The first London squares were built in the 17th century, when landowners decided to develop parts of their estates as places, rather than just streets. The first of these was Covent Garden, a place of recreation as well as a market. This was soon followed by Leicester Square. During the 18th century, 15 squares were built in London to provide elegant town dwellings for the upper-middle classes.

The quality of 18th-century architecture in London has to do with the natural blending of dignified façades with semi-formal landscapes. Bedford Square, started in 1776, with its central garden of grass, shrubs, and plane trees, was the first complete square in London to be arranged in this manner. It has remained more or less intact to this day. Originally, the entire square was a private place, sealed off from the general public by large gates. These elegant gardens reached their designed maturity years after the world they represented had disappeared.

city. Wren concentrated on rebuilding the 50 destroyed churches, providing a new skyline of delicate spires, and a new St. Paul's Cathedral with a lofty dome. At the same time, new regulations were introduced, with tighter controls on materials and building heights.

By 1700, London and its environs had grown to 674,000 people. As building expanded constantly outward from the City, a second bridge over the river was added at Westminster in 1750. Some years later, Blackfriars Bridge was built within the City boundary.

From the start, the Thames had been London's natural gateway, but by the 1820s new docks, shipyards, and wharves were being built downstream of the City. With the coming of the Industrial Revolution, the capital's living environment deteriorated rapidly. The air was filthy with coal smoke, the river was a vast sewer, and crime was rising rapidly. Yet at the same time, in the less crowded areas to the west of the City, elegant streets and squares were being laid out. The Georgian period, roughly corresponding to the reign of King George III from 1760 to 1820, gave rise to London's finest domestic architecture.

Coping with a megalopolis

As the 19th century advanced, London was becoming unbearably congested. New river crossings were needed: Waterloo Bridge in 1817, a new, wider London Bridge in 1832, Hammersmith Bridge in 1887, and Tower Bridge – London's enduring symbol – com-

ARCHITECTS AND LONDON

London owes its classical image above all to Inigo Jones, who regarded the Renaissance style as the only civilized form of architecture. His Banqueting Hall of 1619 was the first truly classical building in the capital. After the fire of 1666, Sir Christopher Wren spread the message with more than 70 buildings, including St. Paul's Cathedral and the Royal Hospital, Chelsea.

In the 18th century, one of the greatest influences was Lord Burlington, a gifted amateur whose chief surviving work, Chiswick House, was based on Palladio's Villa Rotonda. In the era of rapid development at the end of the century, few contributed more than the Adam brothers. Robert Adam, in particular, added a rich variety of Roman decorative features to create his own classical manner.

Undoubtedly the greatest architect-planner was the 19th-century John Nash. He placed sweeping curves of elegant neoclassical rows of houses around the formal landscaping of Regent's Park and renovated Buckingham Palace.

The Gothic revival movement later in the century, led by Augustus Pugin, sought to recreate the purity of Gothic architecture, with its emphasis on bulk and decoration. In the process, London's buildings changed from pale creams and musty grays to blooms of red-brick and terracotta – none more fantastic than Sir George Gilbert-Scott's St. Pancras Station.

The city owes its architectural richness to a continuous replenishment of building ideas. Large modern complexes, such as the Lloyds building, by Sir Richard Rogers, and the ship-like Ark in West London, represent a long, innovative tradition.

The Royal Courts of Justice in the Strand (left, begun 1874) were the culmination of the Gothic Revival style in public building.

Sir Christopher Wren produced a clear and spacious plan for London after the Great Fire which was rejected as too radical.

Rebuilding, especially to repair the bomb damage of World War II and during the expansive Sixties, led to some fine buildings designed by contemporary architects. Public housing projects, planned to overcome severe housing shortages, gave rise to insoluble problems and are now being torn down. More than in the past, London's stock of older buildings is appreciated. Victorian buildings are being refurbished and divided into apartments. To the east along the river, the Docklands area, the largest urban renewal project in Europe, dominated by the tower of Canary Wharf, has aimed to provide for growth along a revitalized waterfront. Once again, London is contemplating a new beginning on the banks of the Thames, this time at the dawn of the 21st century.

The first estate to be developed, Covent Garden, was planned by Inigo Jones, who also designed St. Paul's Church, pictured here.

pleted in 1894. In 1829 the omnibus was introduced, followed by the London and Greenwich Railway some ten years later. To the then fringe of the capital, six major stations were added. London also introduced the world's first underground railroad in 1854. Trams first ran in 1859.

Massive renewal projects were to follow. Wide new thoroughfares such as Shaftesbury Avenue and Southwark Street were thrust upon the capital. This and the building of railroads through poor districts drove many inhabitants to settle elsewhere in cramped conditions.

As commerce grew in volume, the five great London markets became centers of distribution. To meet the new demands on an expanding capital, these central markets sold produce brought in from the surrounding countryside, often to be purchased for consumption in the suburbs near where it had been grown in the first place. Many of these 19th century structures, such as Covent Garden and Billingsgate, are now prized conservation areas, under new management and use, while the markets themselves have moved to less crowded outlying districts.

In 1851, The Great Exhibition was held in a vast, radically new prefabricated structure of cast iron and glass in Hyde Park. It marked the high point of the British Empire, and London, the heart of that empire, was the richest, most populous city in the world. More buildings were constructed during the 19th century than in all the previous ages together.

London continued to spread into suburbs, leapfrogging over the rural Green Belt which had been imposed around it to control growth.

The Barbican was built over the wartime ruins of the City. At its center is an arts complex surrounded by facilities and housing to attract people to the core of the City.

WASHINGTON, D.C.

*A French soldier creates an ideal city for a new nation –
a capital designed in ten months.*

KEY

☐ *Extent of L'Enfant's plan, 1791*

☐ *Reconstruction area*

❶ *Capitol*
❷ *White House*
❸ *The Mall*
❹ *Washington Monument*
❺ *Pentagon*
❻ *Kennedy Center*
❼ *Lincoln Memorial*
❽ *Arlington National Cemetry*
❾ *Pennsylvania Avenue*

Designated by an Act of Congress, Washington, D.C., was the first modern city to be planned on an entirely new site. As a center of the Federal Government – the President, Congress, and the Supreme Court – the city, with its echoes of European baroque veiled in neoclassicism, displays simple dignity on a grand scale. It is only in recent decades that Washington has expanded beyond its original plan, but its center retains the clarity of the original concept.

George Washington (left) and Charles L'Enfant (centre) inspect the site.

After the War of Independence, the new United States of America needed a capital. The project for this Federal District was put in hand with remarkable speed. It was required that, by the first Monday in December 1800, there were to be suitable buildings to accommodate the President and Congress, and a whole range of public buildings. Until that time, the capital was to be in Philadelphia.

Early in 1791, President George Washington appointed three Commissioners and two surveyors, one of whom was Major Pierre-Charles L'Enfant, a French volunteer who served under Washington during the Revolution.

L'Enfant was the son of a court painter at Louis XVI's court at Versailles. He studied at the Royal Academy of Painting and Sculpture in Paris, but gained an army commission as a military engineer. In 1777, at the age of 23, he arrived in America with the colonial troops of the Continental Army. At the battle of Savannah, he was captured by the British.

After the war, he put his artistic training, his knowledge of the great buildings of Paris and Versailles, and his engineering skills to use.

Planning the new capital

The Residential Act of July 1790 authorized President Washington to select a site of

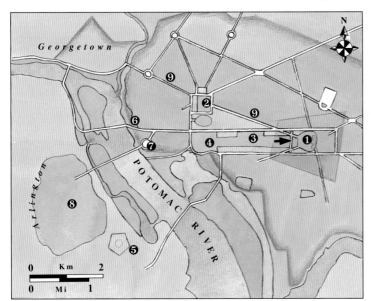

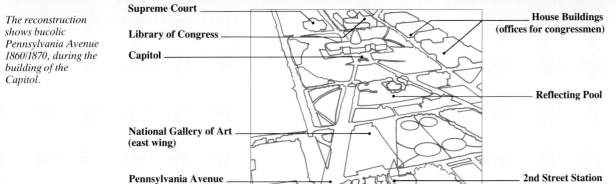

The reconstruction shows bucolic Pennsylvania Avenue 1860/1870, during the building of the Capitol.

Supreme Court

Library of Congress

Capitol

House Buildings
(offices for congressmen)

Reflecting Pool

National Gallery of Art
(east wing)

Pennsylvania Avenue

2nd Street Station

100 square miles along the Potomac River for the autonomous Federal capital. The land he chose included the ports of Alexandria in Virginia and Georgetown in Maryland. Apart from two other small settlements, the area was a swampy malarial wilderness. Today the District of Columbia is two-thirds of its original size. In 1846, the port of Alexandria and the rest of the District south of the Potomac were returned to Virginia.

L'Enfant's expertise in planning fortifications was admired by Washington, who commissioned him to prepare plans for the new capital. Working at remarkable speed – without a contract or a budget – L'Enfant completed site surveys and a first draft of the plan within six months. But not long after, he quarrelled with the Commissioners over the design, embarrassed the President, and was dismissed. By then, however, his farsighted plans were so

well advanced that the new city was realized nine years later.

L'Enfant first established the principal building locations and squares, which he connected by diagonal lines of broad avenues within a grid of streets. The avenues broke the monotony of the regular blocks and provided wide prospects along the alignments. They were also a logical solution to reducing distances, and thus travel time, between focal points. L'Enfant believed that the location of key buildings where the diagonals converged would encourage the city to take form evenly.

A city planner's dream come true

L'Enfant and Washington rode out together to inspect the site. On a ridge overlooking the Potomac, they chose a location for the President's house. About a mile away, at Jenkins Hill, L'Enfant pointed to "a pedestal waiting for a monument" – the site of the future Capitol. These nodes were to be connected by the principal diagonal, Pennsylvania Avenue, and to the Potomac by the Mall, intended to be crowded with people and lined with noble buildings, like the Champs Elysées in Paris. It could, said L'Enfant, "give Washington a superiority of [amenities] over most of the cities of the world."

To Europeans, this vision seemed outrageous. Charles Dickens, on a visit in 1842, described a city of "spacious avenues that begin in nothing and lead nowhere, streets a mile long that only want houses . . . and inhabitants."

The very scale of such a plan, covering some 60,000 acres, was unprecedented. Intended for a population of 120,000, the District of Columbia only had about 50,000 inhabitants in 1846. Small groups of houses were built close to the principal buildings, while, in the

The principal diagonal was Pennsylvania Avenue, a ceremonial boulevard from the Capitol to the White House.

Washington, shown in this 1830 sketch (top), grew slowly. Small groups of houses were built close to major buildings and cattle grazed on the Mall.

THE MALL

The Mall was a central feature in the overall plan for the city. By bringing into the design the topography of the land and the expanse of the river, L'Enfant aimed to combine the natural qualities of the site with an imposing layout of key buildings. He proposed an L-shaped green corridor 400 feet wide, leading from the Capitol building to an equestrian statue of George Washington where the Mall crossed the view south from the White House. Instead, the Washington Monument, an obelisk 550 feet tall, was eventually erected. Since the subsoil on the site was weak, it had to be placed slightly off the axis to guarantee that it was built on a firm foundation.

It took many decades for L'Enfant's intentions to be realized. At first, the area was simply enclosed and used for grazing cattle. By the 1840s, it had become a park with meandering paths. Later, careless planning allowed rail tracks to be laid across it. Early in 1901, after the capital's centenary, the Senate authorized the District Committee to prepare plans for the improvement of the park system in the city, including the Mall. As the central feature of the plan, the Mall was extended to the banks of the Potomac.

The asymmetrical placing of the Washington Monument was resolved by tilting the Capitol axis of the Mall and by adding rows of trees. On the west side, a point reference was made with the Capitol by placing the Lincoln Memorial close to the Potomac; and reflected in a pool, the

The Mall, completed after 100 years, was extended to the banks of the Potomac, close to the Lincoln Memorial. This obelisk links the Capitol with the White House.

Jefferson Memorial was sited on the White House axis, to the south.

The problem of the rail tracks across the Mall was resolved by building a tunnel north of the Capitol, leading to Union Station, which was built in 1908. Today, nearly 200 years after Washington, D.C., was built, the Mall's dignity is assured, altered by only minor deviations from L'Enfant's original plan.

early years, many designated squares were used as vegetable gardens and streets were planted with crops along their alignments.

After World War II, this quiet but imposing city of the South began to change. The Pentagon, the largest single building in the world, was built as the headquarters of the US armed forces. Universities have been founded, galleries built, and the Kennedy Center for the Performing Arts established. National and international agencies rub shoulders with centers of political and industrial power.

In contrast to most modern cities, the center of Washington is inhabited by an élite group of officials and businesspeople, while the suburbs have become home to the disadvantaged. But whatever demographic problems the city faces, its gracious design and buildings present a confident face to the nation and the world at large.

Georgetown, near the Capitol, reflects the architectural style of colonial America, although few original houses survive.

SYDNEY

In barely two centuries, a collection of tents for convicts has grown into a city of skyscrapers, famed for its unique Opera House.

Sydney lies on one of the most beautiful sites in the world, spreading out expansively between the sea and the mountains. The city has developed from a penal settlement of tents and shacks to one of the largest metropolitan areas in the world, equally famed for its innovative buildings and its vivid lifestyle. Sydney's dynamism owes much to the way the city has been allowed to grow over the 200 years since it was founded.

The world's finest harbor

Inland Australian Aborigines had to endure the harsh climate of an arid land, but the first people to come to the bay on the southeast coast found a paradise with rivers and abundant vegetation. It had been untroubled by foreign visitors for 60,000 years. In 1606, the master of the Dutch ship *Duyfken* first sighted the northern coast of what became known as *terra australis incognita*, the unknown southern land. Yet the southeast remained inviolate until April 29, 1770, when Captain James Cook in his ship HMS *Endeavour* came ashore at a place he called Botany Bay, after the wealth of new plants discovered there by

Captain James Cook came ashore on April 29, 1770, at a landing point which he called Botany Bay.

his botanist, Joseph Banks. Cook later named the land New South Wales and claimed it for King George III. Cook glimpsed another inlet and named it Port Jackson after the Judge-Advocate of the Royal Navy, Sir George Jackson, but did not enter what would be described 18 years later as "the finest harbor in the world."

The British Government was concerned over the loss in 1776 of its American colonies as a place for the disposal of criminals. The remote

From its beginnings as a prison colony, Sydney has spread to embrace some 600 suburbs, making the city one of the most extensive in the world.

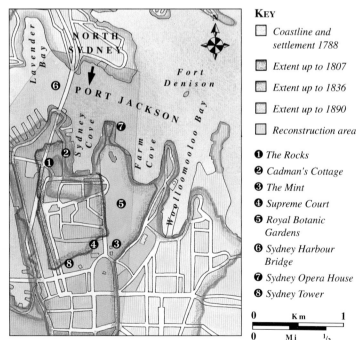

KEY

☐ *Coastline and settlement 1788*

☐ *Extent up to 1807*

☐ *Extent up to 1836*

☐ *Extent up to 1890*

☐ *Reconstruction area*

❶ *The Rocks*
❷ *Cadman's Cottage*
❸ *The Mint*
❹ *Supreme Court*
❺ *Royal Botanic Gardens*
❻ *Sydney Harbour Bridge*
❼ *Sydney Opera House*
❽ *Sydney Tower*

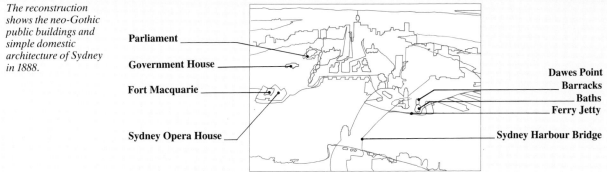

The reconstruction shows the neo-Gothic public buildings and simple domestic architecture of Sydney in 1888.

Parliament

Government House

Fort Macquarie

Sydney Opera House

Dawes Point

Barracks

Baths

Ferry Jetty

Sydney Harbour Bridge

new colony seemed a perfect substitute. In May 1787, the first fleet of 11 ships set sail from Portsmouth. Travelling 14,000 miles via Cape Town, it arrived at Botany Bay on January 20 the following year. Under the command of Captain Arthur Phillip and 211 marines (together with 41 members of their families), there were 736 criminals: 548 men and 188 women, and 17 children (six of them born on the way). The first landing site was sandy, exposed, and unsuitable for a settlement, so Captain Phillip sailed around the headland to Port Jackson.

The penal colony

On January 26 the birth of Australia became official when muskets were fired and the Union Jack was hoisted close to the future site of the Customs House (built about 100 years later). The new township was sited on Sydney Cove, named after the Home Secretary Thomas Townshend Lord Sydney. A makeshift residence was hastily erected for Captain Phillip, who was the first Governor of New South Wales. The convicts were housed in tents a short distance away at the Rocks, on

the opposite side of Sydney Cove from the site of the present Opera House. Soon the tents were replaced with wooden huts, then more permanent buildings.

Conditions in the early days were harsh, and the new colony faced starvation until supply ships arrived. The second fleet came in 1790, with the third fleet in the following year, bringing the first Irish convicts ashore. The population was now nearly 3,000.

Discipline was swiftly enforced by flogging or the gallows. At the same time, the Governor took every opportunity to pardon criminals and provide them with a small piece of land to feed themselves. Convicts were paroled for good behavior and encouraged to marry. Many took the opportunity to improve their circumstances. Francis Greenway, convicted of forgery, was to become Sydney's leading architect. Mary Reibey, transported for horse theft at the age of 13, went on to make her

This view of Sydney Cove in 1804 shows the town spreading, thanks to free settlers who arrived from Britain after 1793 to take up land.

fortune as a businesswoman.

From 1793 on, free settlers began to arrive from Britain to take up tempting offers of land. In 1806, Captain William Bligh, the former commander of HMS *Bounty,* was made Governor of New South Wales, until he was overthrown by a rebellion in 1808. His successor, Governor Lachlan Macquarie, was to govern wisely for 12 years from 1810. In the same year, 9,300 men and 2,500 women were transported.

Planning for a hot climate

At an early stage, a town plan was laid out. The main streets were to be 200 feet wide "to admit a free circulation of air." Only one

Some convicts were able to receive pardons and found an opportunity to improve their circumstances.

SYDNEY'S FIRST ARCHITECT

Until 1814, Sydney did not have an architect. Buildings were simple, mainly single-story structures. In 1814, Francis Greenway, a skilled architect, was transported to Sydney Cove for forgery. Working closely with Governor Macquarie, who had a passion for architecture, he designed the new city's principal buildings.

Greenway's first building, a lighthouse at the harbor entrance, won him a conditional pardon, and his elegant convict barracks in Macquarie Street earned him full freedom. In his six years as official architect for the colony, he single-handedly produced 40 buildings, 11 of them, including the fine St James's Church off Macquarie Street, still standing. His face appeared on the first Australian $10 bill – a rare distinction for a forger.

Francis Greenaway (1777–1837), a convicted forger, was pardoned in 1816 and became Sydney's architect.

house was to be built on each allotment of 60 × 120 feet. The Georgian style was modified for the Sydney climate: wide, two-story houses were surrounded by verandas. By 1819, the town seemed to a French visitor a thriving European city, all the more striking for its isolation.

During the 19th century, the earliest area of settlement became Sydney's trade and commerce center. It was now an overcrowded, insanitary, and violent district. Until the first bank was established in 1817, rum was effectively the colony's currency. Sydney's oldest building, Cadman's Cottage, erected in 1816 as barracks for the colony's boat crew, still stands here. It is named after John Cadman, transported from Britain for horse stealing and pardoned in 1814 to become a coxswain. Other colonial buildings have survived in the surrounding Argyle Street, Bridge Street, and George Street. What became Parliament House was built between 1810 and 1816 with a tasteful colonnaded façade. In 1810, a park was designated by the new Governor, and the

The Rocks was the site of the first convict tents in 1788. The area contains many examples of colonial Georgian buildings and old warehouses.

colony's first substantial farm was established on the site of the Royal Botanic Gardens.

With prosperity came new social classes, with the "exclusives" (descendants of troops and free immigrants) at the top of the tree. But skills were also needed. From 1840, New South Wales took no more transported criminals; instead, tradesmen and craftsmen were encouraged to settle in the colony.

Sydney University was founded in 1850, a sign of the new city's development. Between 1831 and 1850, some 200,000 immigrants fled the misery of 19th-century Britain to Sydney's southern sunshine. By 1870, Sydney was a prosperous port with a population of 288,000. New public buildings were erected in a Gothic revival style. Domestic architecture remained simple and unpretentious, as can still be seen in the row of houses of Kings Cross. Verandas decorated with intricate wrought-iron "lace" give this architecture a distinctively Australian flavor. The iron, made in Britain, was brought over as ballast in ships which left laden with produce such as frozen meat, which Australia began to export in 1880.

The expansive city

In the 20th century, suburbs spread extensively around the estuaries of the Parramatta and Georges rivers. By 1925, the population of Sydney had reached 1 million. Today there are more than 3.5 million people in Greater Sydney. Some 600 suburbs lie between the Pacific Ocean to the east, the Blue Mountains to the west, and national parks north and south. Sydney has spread over an area of 700 square miles. Although not as large as Los Angeles, it is one of the most extensive cities in the world.

The harbor divides the city into two halves, with business and industry in the south down

SYDNEY OPERA HOUSE

The Sydney Opera House in its waterside location has become *the instantly recognizable symbol of the city.*

Sydney Opera House has become the city's symbol in the 20 years since it was opened by Queen Elizabeth II in 1973. The Opera House has three linked sections covering 4.4 acres, seating more than 5,100 people. It stands on the site once occupied by Fort Macquarie.

The Opera House was designed by the Danish architect Jørn Utzon. He envisioned an extraordinary construction of concrete "sails," their surfaces forming a continuously varying curve in two dimensions. It proved impossible to make molds for them, and eventually – after 16 years of planning – the shape was approximated by using segments of a sphere. Construction, and completion of the interior, took another 14 years.

SYDNEY HARBOR BRIDGE

Before the construction of the Bridge, the only way to cross the Harbor was by ferry. In the 1920s, there were some 70 ferries constantly crossing between the city and the North Shore. With an increasing population and use of cars, a bridge became a necessity.

The Bridge was designed by the Australian engineer J. J. C. Bradfield and the British Sir Ralph Freeman. The immense girders were forged in Yorkshire in England and shipped out. Construction began in 1923 and took almost nine years.

It was the largest girder span in the world, 1,650 feet long and 160 feet wide. There are eight traffic lanes, two rail lanes, a bicycle path, and a walkway. The top of "the coat hanger," as the Bridge is known to local people, is 436 feet above the water. The steelwork takes ten years to repaint.

The Bridge carries some 160,000 vehicles each day. Even this has proved inadequate: traffic congestion has now required the construction of a tunnel under the Harbor, providing an alternative route between northern and eastern suburbs.

to Botany Bay and north over the Bridge into the residential areas. Some of the fashionable districts, such as Darling Point and Vaucluse, are on the east side, overlooking the Pacific. People living along the deeply indented, 160-mile-long coastline in the waterside suburbs are likely to have a boat at the end of their backyards. There are more than 30 beaches.

Until recently, wealthy Australians lived in the spacious outer suburbs, leaving the center to new immigrants from Greece, Italy, and other European countries, and increasingly from the Far East. Now some 30 percent of Sydney's population was born outside Australia. A new generation of Australians is returning to the center and renovating the historic inner districts that their grandparents once abandoned.

The harbor divides the city into two parts, and the suburbs sprawl north and south along the coast and east and west to the mountains.

MOSCOW

A European city, but the capital of an empire that once stretched to the Pacific, Moscow stands apprehensively on the brink of a new era.

Moscow stands at the crossroads of Europe and Asia. A capital city since the 15th century, it has looked to Western Europe for cultural inspiration. However, feudalism survived in Russia effectively up to the time of the October Revolution of 1917, centuries after its demise in the rest of Europe, and this is reflected in medieval street patterns that survive to the present day. In contrast, the authoritarian urban forms of wide avenues and monumental

KEY

- ▣ Assumed extent of Kremlin and Kitay Gorod in 1538
- ▨ The two defensive walls in 1606
- ▦ Extent in 1935
- ▢ Reconstruction area

❶ Kremlin
❷ Cathedral of the Ascension
❸ Red Square
❹ Lenin's Mausoleum
❺ St. Basil's Cathedral
❻ Tsentrosoyuz Building
❼ Russian Parliament

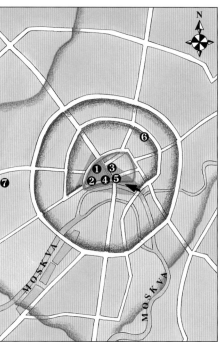

architecture express the power of the state in the Soviet Socialist empire. Today, with the collapse of Communism, Moscow faces a transitional period, replacing stagnation with uncertainty, as Moscovites struggle in the face of political and economic chaos.

The Ministry of Foreign Affairs building shows the ornate style of the Stalinist era, with its tall towers and predominantly Gothic ornament.

A fort on the river

Commanding a prominent position on the river Moskva, Moscow occupies a central position close to major water routes. There was a settlement on the area around the Kremlin (which means "high town") before the 12th century. Kucho, a local boyar (chieftain), occupied a stronghold close to the river. In 1147, Yuri Dolgorukiy, who became Prince of

The reconstruction shows the view looking up the Moskva River towards the Kremlin, 1880/1890.

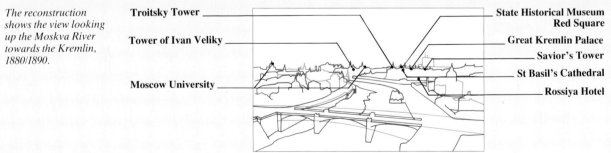

Troitsky Tower

Tower of Ivan Veliky

Moscow University

State Historical Museum
Red Square

Great Kremlin Palace

Savior's Tower

St Basil's Cathedral

Rossiya Hotel

Suzdal in 1149, transferred the settlement to a wooden fort on a ridge 150 feet above the river, between the left bank of the Moskva and the Neglinnaia tributary. The new settlement developed on the western part of the hill, at first over an area of some 10 acres. Over the next two centuries, it grew to cover 75 acres.

The first Prince of Moscow was Daniil (reigned 1276–1303), son of Alexander Nevsky. He and his successors strove to make the city a major stronghold, and the Kremlin became the political and administrative core of the city. The stone Cathedral of the Assumption in the Kremlin was built during the mid-14th century. In 1367, defenses were improved by the construction of masonry walls around the fort. The present high walls, strengthened by some 20 towers, were completed in 1508. An outer wooden wall ran along the present Bul'varnoye Kol'tso and included the monasteries of St. Peter, the Nativity, and the Stetenskiy.

The capital of Russia

When, in 1472, Grand Prince Ivan III (1462–1505) married Sophia Paleologus, the niece of the last Byzantine Emperor, he declared Moscow the "Third Rome." He incorporated the double-headed eagle of the Byzantine Empire in the Muscovite arms, at the same time declaring himself head of the whole Orthodox Church.

The status of Moscow further increased when, in 1480, Ivan defeated the Mongol Tartars and declared himself Autocrat of all Russia. From the 15th century on, the development of an essentially Russian architecture was led by Moscow. The cathedrals and fortifications of the modern Kremlin date mainly from this period.

Ivan III's grandson, the notorious Ivan the

THE KREMLIN

The Kremlin, covering an area of some 70 acres, was the citadel for the Church and the stronghold of the Muscovite princes. The center around which Moscow developed, it became the seat of the Soviet government. It is now visited daily by 60,000 tourists.

The wooden walls were 10 feet high, with double gates and tall towers. The present stone walls, 1½ miles in length, up to 65 feet high and more than 20 feet thick, date from the 15th century, during the reign of Ivan III. The magnificent Cathedral Square dates from the 14th century. Numerous palaces, cathedrals, and cloisters were built at the peak of Russian power during the 16th and 17th centuries. The early court style was fused with the Italianate Renaissance style to produce awe-inspiring buildings whose huge walls and gilt onion domes have come to symbolize the whole city.

The Cathedral of the Annunciation (1484–89), with its nine richly decorated golden domes, stands next to the Great Kremlin Palace.

Terrible (1533–84), was the first ruler of Russia to be crowned Tsar (emperor). He commissioned the building of St. Basil's Cathedral to commemorate his capture of the Kazan stronghold from the Volga Tartars in 1552.

By the mid-16th century, Moscow was one of the largest cities in Europe, with a population of some 100,000. The city grew outward, ringed by groups of fortified monasteries. The commercial part to the east of the Kremlin lay outside the moat in the area known as Kitay Gorod (which also includes the modern Red Square). This, together with the Kremlin, formed the nucleus of the city. An outer wooden wall 10 miles long was hastily built to counter a threat of invasion from the Tartars. This wall, now overlaid by the present second ring road (Sadovoye Kol'tso), was later rebuilt in stone, and remained the city boundary until the 17th century.

Tsar Mikhail (1613–45) was the first of the Romanov dynasty, which ruled Russia for more than 300 years. By 1663, Moscow had more than 200 churches. In addition, the city

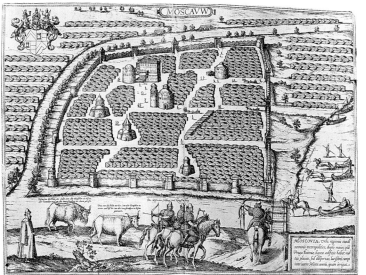

At the time of this engraving, the mid-16th century, Moscow was one of the largest cities in Europe, with a population of 100,000.

This winter scene by A. Cadolle (1826–70) shows the Moskva River and the Kremlin beyond with its splendid brick walls and towers.

tant industrial center in Russia. There were around 500 churches, and increasingly brick and stone were being used to build houses. The city was also a green place, with wide tree-lined boulevards; some 10 percent of the urban area was devoted to gardens and parklands.

The Revolution and after

As early as the reign of Alexander II (1855–81), reforms were introduced to placate opposition to the rigid social order imposed by successive Tsars. But little attempt was being made to deal with the difficult living conditions of the working people. From the 1890s, Marxism was a growing force.

When the Revolution came in 1917, it was more violent in Moscow than in Petrograd (as St. Petersburg was now called). Gunfire broke

was a commercial center with a bustling marketplace. It was divided into quarters for the nobility, merchants, artisans, and foreigners. People lived in wooden houses and fires were frequent, destroying the city several times.

While St. Petersburg, founded by Peter the Great (1682–1725), bloomed into a magnificent city, Moscow played the greater role in the development of Russia. From the 1740s, a grandiose architecture symbolized its might.

When Napoleon invaded Russia, Moscow was one of his main objectives. After the battle at Borodino in 1812, 68 miles to the west, Napoleon established his headquarters in the Kremlin – but found no one to surrender the city to him. As fire destroyed some 80 percent of the houses, Napoleon withdrew from the smoldering ruins.

By the end of the 19th century, Moscow grew to become the second largest city in Europe, after London. By 1912, it had a population of 1.5 million and was the most impor-

RED SQUARE

Red Square lies outside the northeastern wall of the Kremlin. It was so named long before the emergence of communism: the Russian word *krasny* means both "red" and "beautiful." The gigantic space covers 18 acres. As part of the Kitay Gorod, Moscow's first suburb, it is one of the oldest areas in the city and became the nucleus of its trading center. The world-renowned GUM department store, on the north side of Red Square, continues the tradition of commerce to this day.

Since 1550, when Ivan the Terrible used it for some of his most violent excesses, Red Square has been the scene of many disturbances. The first shots of the Bolshevik uprising were fired in Red Square.

Under the Soviets, the square became famous for the military parades held on May Day and the anniversary of the October Bolshevik Revolution. Here also, close to the northern wall of the Kremlin, is the bulky Lenin Mausoleum in granite, designed by the architect A. V. Shchuser. At the southeastern end of the square is the Cathedral of the Virgin of the Intercession by the Moat, known throughout the world as St. Basil's Cathedral, with its multicolored cupolas.

St. Basil's Cathedral, with its multicolored central dome encircled *by eight smaller ones, was commissioned by Ivan the Terrible.*

It was commissioned by Ivan the Terrible to commemorate his capture of Kazan from the Tartars on the day of the Feast of the Intercession. Designed by the architect Posnik Yakovlev, it was erected between 1555 and 1560. Originally painted red and white, with green domes (as were many provincial churches), it was given its present multicolored decoration in the 17th century. This has made it an unforgettable sight, one of the most famous buildings in the world.

out in many streets. During March 1918, Lenin (head of state 1917–24) transferred the Soviet government from Petrograd to Moscow. By 1920, a mass exodus of Muscovites to the countryside almost halved the 1.9 million population of 1917. But as Stalin (1927–53) consolidated his power, the cities, including Moscow, benefited from economic growth. By 1939, Moscow's population had rebounded to 4.2 million. Stalin's 1935 plan of reconstruction for Moscow was on an unprecedented scale. Many major avenues were laid out; the famous Metro was built and decorated with cascading crystal chandeliers and imposing statues of workers; and vast public buildings in "Stalin Gothic" style embellished the city.

A major event in World War II was the Battle for Moscow, marking the first major defeat for Hitler and the first Soviet triumph. German forces came within 20 miles of the city, but did not enter it. Much of the surrounding area was laid waste, with enormous human suffering.

After the war, the urban pattern of Moscow changed dramatically. Vast new housing

Chudow Monastery (shown damaged by shrapnel in 1917) was *demolished by Stalin in 1932 to make way for the Presidium.*

The basic ingredients in the Moscow skyline are the massive balls and gilt onion domes, with monolithic tower blocks in the distance.

projects, such as Novyye Chevyomustiki, were built on the periphery of the capital. A drab and monotonous development of five-story buildings was superceded by a variety of developments, visually dominated by tall towers. A distinctive neighborhood layout, the *mikrovayon,* or small district consisting of groups of apartments with shops, became the standard dwelling unit in Moscow.

By 1961, Moscow had extended outside its ring of superhighways. In 1980, the city was host to the Olympic Games. Large sports facilities were built, together with the Olympic Village, now a housing project.

From 1985, the rule of Mikhail Gorbachev instituted a policy of *glasnost* (openness) and *perestroika* (reconstruction), effectively bringing communism and the Soviet Union itself to an end. Today, Moscow is the capital of the Russian Federation. It stands on the threshold of another period of change and development. The sprawling metropolis of 8.5 million people now covers nearly 620 square miles, four times its size in 1917. Yet among the drab housing projects much of Old Moscow survives.

MOSCOW'S ARCHITECTURE

The centralization begun by Ivan III in the 15th century made Moscow the focus of Russian architecture. The traditional style of wooden church created a soaring space over a relatively small area, the roof pitched like a steep tent. Corbeled vaulting was a later innovation.

A simple form of church architecture, devised with the help of Italian architects, raised the building on a podium to create the impression of isolation. This style, developed using brick instead of stone, meant buildings could be erected more economically and more quickly.

Grand Prince Ivan III, Ruler of All Russia.

The Italian architect Aristotele Fiororanti created the distinctive five-domed Cathedral of the Assumption (1475–79). This style was adopted in the 17th century to promote traditional Russian architecture. The resulting hybrid, Russian Baroque, can be seen in the monasteries of the time, in the ornate stone pilasters and white window frames.

By the 1850s, competing traditional and innovative architects gave Moscow an eclectic style which found expression in such disparate buildings as the Bolshoi Theater (1856), the Pushkin Fine Arts Museum (1898–1912), and the Central Telegraph Office (1927). Constructivism, which rejected conventional decoration, emerged in the 1920s to reflect new materials and construction techniques. It was seen in the workers' clubs and was used by P. A. Golosov for the Pravda offices (1929–35) and for Le Corbusier's Tsentrosoyuz building (1929–36).

Much of the center of Moscow is dominated by massive ornate buildings erected in the 1930s–50s in the "Stalin Gothic" style, most famously the Metro stations. In 1955, under Khrushchev, a decree forbade the use of expensive layouts and extravagant decoration. The international style was officially adopted by the Soviets, as in the Kremlin Palace of Congress (1961) by Mikhail Posokhin.

The Bolshoi Theater was redesigned by Albert Cavos with a columned façade and a quadriga bearing a statue of Apollo.

TOKYO

In the city's frantic rush hour, strong men are employed to push commuters into packed train cars – with the utmost politeness.

In any other culture, Tokyo would be hell on earth: 25 million people shoulder to shoulder, prices almost beyond belief, and earth tremors an everyday event. Japanese discipline and community spirit make it work.

The Shogun's castle

In 1456, a warlord built a castle on the site of the present Imperial Palace, near the small fishing village of Edo ("estuary gate") on the west bank of the Sumida River. In

At one time the largest castle in the world, then occupied by the Tokugawa Shoguns, it became the Imperial Palace in 1868 and is now entered by way of the Nijubashi bridge.

1590, Toyotomi Hideyoshi, one of the unifiers of Japan, appointed Tokugawa Ieyasu to rule eight provinces. Ieyasu established himself at Edo Castle. In 1601, he became Shogun (generalissimo) of all Japan and founded the Tokugawa shogunate, which was to last until 1867. Although Japan was nominally ruled by an Emperor living in Kyoto, the Shogun had the real civil power.

Ieyasu rebuilt the castle in magnificent style,

The perfect symmetry of the sacred mountain Fuji, reflected in Lake Yamanaka, dominates the view from Tokyo 62 miles away. It has inspired artists and poets throughout the city's history.

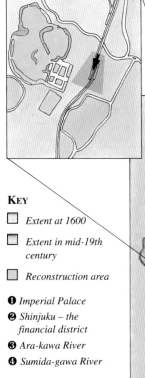

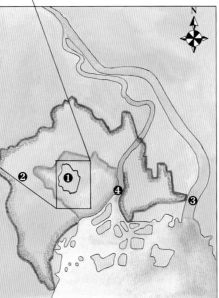

KEY

☐ Extent at 1600

☐ Extent in mid-19th century

☐ Reconstruction area

❶ Imperial Palace

❷ Shinjuku – the financial district

❸ Ara-kawa River

❹ Sumida-gawa River

*The reconstruction
shows the view along
Nihombashi Road in
1909. The contrast
reveals the extent of
rebuilding in Tokyo in
the last eighty years.*

with the tallest tower in Japan. It was not finished until 1640, 24 years after his death. Around it a large city grew up.

The first plan of Edo was based on Japan's ancient capital, Kyoto, itself based on the Chinese city of Cha'gau, laid out in accordance with the Chinese magical art of geomancy. When Edo became the civil capital in 1603, Ieyasu adopted a bold new layout, with waterways for defense and transportation stretching between the castle and the river. Land was reclaimed from the estuary, but for strategic reasons the river was not bridged.

In 1657, fire destroyed the castle and most of the city and its 107,000 inhabitants. Edo was soon rebuilt, on a more open plan to avoid the spread of fire, and with widely separated residences for the samurai (warrior nobles). The first bridge, Ryogokubasi, was built in 1660; others followed.

The "High City," including the new castle and the samurai estates, occupied 60 percent of the land. A further 20 percent was devoted to temples and shrines, chief among these the Kanei-ji Temple in what is now Ueno Park, built in 1624. This was destroyed in the 19th century in the battles which ended the shogunate.

The outer region of the city, Shitamachi ("low land"), a reclaimed marsh covering the remaining area but accommodating more than half the population, was for commoners. It was divided into areas for different trades, a system of which traces survive.

The overhanging roofs of tiered temples were made of wood.

The present Kabuki-za (theater, right) dates from 1925.

The nobility lived in houses along broad streets such as those shown in the print (below), but commoners occupied waste ground.

Nihombashi still has many buildings where stocks and shares are traded. The present Bank of Japan building is on the site of the gold mint. The Ginza ("silver mint") has become a famous shopping center.

More temples surrounded the city, having a defensive as well as a religious role. These became centers of learning. All commoners were registered at a temple for religious education. The temple gardens provided much-needed open space for the overcrowded city.

The floating world

Numerous officials moved into Edo to handle Japan's vast bureaucratic system. The population was also swelled by the samurai's retainers and hangers-on. The merchant class prospered. All these people sought entertainment, which centered around Yoshiwara, Edo's theater and "red light" district. The name means

"field of reeds"; it was originally on a reclaimed marsh, but after 1657 the district was moved outside the city boundaries.

Yoshiwara is vividly recorded in the woodblock prints known as *ukiyo-e* ("pictures of the floating world"), an art which culminated in the work of the great 19th-century artists Ando Hiroshige, Katsushika Hokusai, and Kitagawa Utamaro. Prints show actors in scenes from the Kabuki theater, daily life, and erotic subjects.

The high cultural period of the mid-18th century was known as Edokko ("children of Edo"). The Shoguns tried to curb the citizens' luxurious life during the 1790s and again in the 1840s, with little effect. By 1860, the population was 1.4 million, and the city covered 18 of its 23 present districts.

The Meiji Restoration

Until 1853, Japan was isolated from the world. Then the United States insisted on opening trading relations, soon followed by other countries. This led to unrest; in 1867, isolationists forced the Shogun Yoshinobu to abdicate. The next year, the Meiji Emperor became the civil ruler. The government gradually evolved closer to Western models – partly to counter the growing influence of the West itself.

The Emperor moved his court from Kyoto to Edo, now renamed Tokyo ("eastern city").

ARCHITECTURE THEN AND NOW

Carved embellishments in wood decorated the original Kannon Temple at Asakusa, destroyed in 1945. The present pagoda was built in 1973 in ferroconcrete.

The distinctive twin towers of the new town hall and metropolitan office complex in the Shinjuku district are the work of architect Kenzo Tange.

Japanese building design has influenced the modern architecture of the West, with features such as non-supporting walls, clear straight lines, and functional simplicity. The size of rooms is a multiple of the standard *tatami* straw floor mat – leading to a repeated unit of standard size.

To offset the boxy appearance of buildings, large overhanging roofs often had curves and elaborate details. The thin walls included many sliding panels, eliminating the boundary between interior and exterior. The yard became a continuation of the house, laid out on the same simple, harmonious lines.

Exposure to the West gradually introduced new influences. Frank Lloyd Wright designed the Imperial Hotel, one of the few buildings to survive the 1923 earthquake. Le Corbusier built a hall in Ueno Park. Oddly, Tokyo's main rail station, built in red brick in 1914, is a replica of Amsterdam's.

Japanese modern architects soon found their own voice. After World War II, Maekawa Kunio won international acclaim; his pupil Kenzo Tange designed the stadium for the 1964 Tokyo Olympics and the 48-story City Hall. In 1972, Kuokawa Kisho built the radical Nakagiu Capsule Tower, with 140 replacable housing units. Others, such as Ando Tadao, used traditional influences.

The castle became the Imperial Palace. The samurai fled to the provinces; their estates were turned into farms.

Japan was now becoming an industrial power, and Tokyo expanded further, extending over the former samurai estates. Attempts to replan the city failed because of conflicts of interests. Meanwhile, conditions became more and more crowded.

Rising from the ashes

The city is in a geologically active area, and small earthquakes are a routine event. In 1707, an eruption of Mount Fuji choked Edo with ash. The most serious quake came in 1923, killing 140,000. In 1945, Allied bombing created a firestorm; a further 100,000 died and most of the city was razed. But the city has always recovered quickly.

The enormous pressure on land remains, however. Even the rich can only afford tiny apartments. The highway network built in the 1960s runs largely above rivers; land was too expensive to buy.

Shinjuku ("new lodgings") was once a settlement on the outskirts of Edo, but it now represents all that is modern in Tokyo.

SAN FRANCISCO

The city by the bay retains an easygoing charm which many modern cities have long since lost.

From its modest beginnings as a small Spanish fort, San Francisco grew explosively with the Gold Rush of 1849, increasing its population eightfold in a single year. Somehow it has managed to remain one of the most beautiful of American cities, sprawling comfortably over a range of steep hills which make its streets a challenge for all forms of transportation. The city is equally famous for its antique, clanging cable cars and its towering Golden Gate Bridge, with a clear span of more than half a mile.

The Presidio

Spanish explorers had traveled along the northern coast of California as early as 1542, when Juan Cabrillo sailed into San Diego Bay. Sir Francis Drake arrived in 1579 at a place now called Drake's Bay, north of the present city, claiming all the lands of the Miwok Indians for Queen Elizabeth I.

It took another 200 years for a European to sail into San Francisco Bay itself, when Juan Manuel de Ayala came in 1775. The following year, Juan Bautista de Anza arrived with 200 soldiers and settlers and established the Presidio of San Francisco, named after St. Francis of Assisi.

A *presidio* was a military community. The Spanish laid out a rectangular enclosure 650 feet long on each side, with 13-foot adobe walls to repulse Indian raids. Inside were the barracks and stables, the church, some shops and

KEY

☐ *Original coastline and Yerba Buena up to 1840*

▨ *Extent by 1849*

▨ *Extent by 1856*

☐ *Reconstruction area*

❶ *Presidio*
❷ *Nob Hill*
❸ *Chinatown*
❹ *Market Street*
❺ *Golden Gate Bridge*
❻ *Ferry Building*
❼ *Transamerica Pyramid*
❽ *Lombard Street*
❾ *Oakland Bay Bridge*

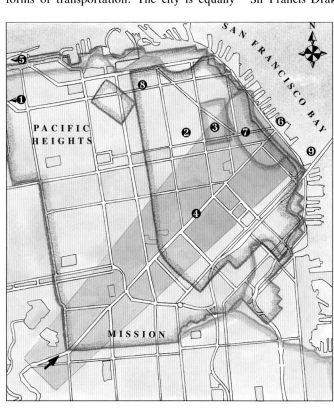

The Gold Rush attracted thousands of prospectors – 49ers – to San Francisco. The population rose from 850 to 6,000 in one year and doubled the following year. This poster advertises a cheap clipper passage to the city.

The reconstruction shows the city reborn: Market Street and the business district c.1916, after the earthquake of 1906.

Bank of America Building

Transamerica Pyramid Building

City Hall

Oakland Bay Bridge

Ferry Building

US Mint

stores, and a few houses for settlers. The buildings were placed against the fort walls, like the area around a cathedral. The houses and farms outside the walls gave the appearance of a civil settlement. A number of the old Presidio buildings still stand today on their original site.

From village to city

In the early 1800s, a small unofficial village called Yerba Buena ("good grass") grew up about 2 miles away, on the natural harbor along the Bay. This formed the beginning of modern San Francisco.

In 1821, the newly independent Mexican state took over the town. In 1846, the Mexican War broke out, and the whole West Coast was captured by the U.S. The Americans took possession of Yerba Buena and a year later

View of San Francisco in 1848.

changed the name to San Francisco.

The town was already well established. In 1839 a Swiss surveyor, Jean-Jacques Vioget, had laid out the first few streets. The settlement had 12 houses for about 50 people. In 1847,

the grid layout was extended by Jasper O'Farrell. At that time, the only open space was the plaza along Kearney Street. From this simple township, San Francisco grew rapidly into a huge, sprawling city.

A few days before the U.S. took control of the settlement, gold had been discovered in the foothills of the Sierra Nevada. When the Gold Rush started, the population was about 850. By the end of 1849, it had reached 6,000, doubling again in the next year. Thousands more people (known as the Forty-Niners) also passed through the city on their way to the gold fields and returned in the winter months.

The Gold Rush had an immediate effect on land values, with prices rising tenfold in a few months. The demand for building sites was met by expanding the grid pattern over a large

THE CABLE CARS

The cable car is known worldwide as one of the symbols of San Francisco. The steep hills made conventional horsedrawn and electric street cars unworkable. The only possible solution with the resources of the late 19th century was to pull the cars up the hills with steel cables. The first cars ran in 1873. At once, they became an essential part of San Francisco's transportation system, encouraging development on the steep hills by providing convenient access to hilly areas. Without them, the city's high society would never have settled on Nob Hill.

The thick cable runs in a slot under the street, going around pulleys at the corners. Originally, the cable was hauled by steam

The first cable cars ran in 1873, encouraging early development on the steep hills. Of more

than 600 cable cars running in 1900, only 40 still function today.

engines in buildings at the end of the line. Now these have been replaced by electric motors. The cable moves continuously. The car can be uncoupled at stops.

Before the 1906 earthquake, more than 600 cable cars traveled over 110 miles across the city. By the mid-1950s, with the increasing use of the motor vehicle, there were only 17 miles of line in use, and plans were being made to close down the system. But by that time they had become an essential part of the city's character, and there were public protests. The cars have continued to run, and the entire system was refurbished in the early 1990s. Today, there are three lines using 40 cars, the steepest one running up Nob Hill.

scribed the streets as being "full of people, hurrying to and fro and of as diverse and bizarre a character as the houses."

Within months of the start of the rush, the grid of streets extended up the hills and down toward the Bay. The chessboard layout provided a sense of order and simplified development, but it ignored the precipitous terrain, with streets running straight up and down the steep hillsides.

San Francisco became a chartered city in 1850. By 1853, the population had reached 50,000. Further extensions were added to the west in 1856, providing six open squares each the size of a city block. Settlement in this area was slow because of the difficult terrain and the distance from the center. However, land within the oldest district developed rapidly. The Golden Gate Park was established, providing a large open space to the west overlooking the Pacific Ocean.

In spite of the seeming monotony of the grid layout, the superb location of San Francisco

area. At first, the town grew within three hills, rising sharply from the water between the Golden Gate to the north, San Francisco Bay to the east, and the Pacific Ocean to the west.

Another grid pattern was started at a 45-degree angle from the original settlement along Market Street, which formed the meeting point between the two separately laid-out segments of the city. The modern business district is concentrated close to this wide street and the spacious Union Square.

Development in the town was frantic and uneven. There were people living in tents, wooden shacks, adobe buildings, and a few more solid structures. Bayard Taylor, who arrived in San Francisco at the time of the Gold Rush and recorded his impressions, de-

A new grid pattern was laid out at a 45-degree angle to the original settlement, with Market Street forming the meeting point between the two.

The buildings on the slopes of the steep hills were left to the whims of individual property owners, as shown here on Telegraph Hill in 1863.

SAN FRANCISCO'S SKYLINE

The rising cost of real estate creates a haphazard skyline.

The attenuated pyramid of the Transamerica Building, erected 20 years ago on Columbus Avenue, created considerable controversy as being inappropriate to San Francisco's skyline. With much of this skyline now partly obliterated, its presence has mellowed, and this 48-story building is now recognized as part of the San Francisco scene.

Through the years, the skyline of San Francisco maintained a relationship between topography and buildings. Tall buildings were placed on the crests of the hills, low buildings on the slopes, thus accentuating the natural profile of the city. At the same time, the panoramic views remained uninterrupted.

In the last 20 years, the cost of real estate and the desire of large corporations to advertise themselves with tall buildings has distorted this simple concept. Unless clear guidelines are adhered to, San Francisco's skyline will become the same as that of any other American city.

The Ferry Building, long San Francisco's most distinctive landmark, made an imposing end to a long vista along Market Street. Now it is lost among the tall skyscrapers of the financial district.

The 48-story Transamerica Building on Columbus Avenue, controversial when it was first built, is now a familiar part of the San Francisco skyline.

proved to be indestructible, offering spectacular views across the Bay and the Pacific Ocean. How best to deal with buildings on the slopes of the steep hills was left to the individual property buyer.

At the start of the 1860s, San Francisco became the terminus of the Pony Express. By the end of the decade, the transcontinental railway, built by imported Chinese labor, had reached the city. San Francisco was a boom town again. This time, the attraction was the abundant silver ore in the mountains of western Nevada. Mining here was on a much larger scale than that at the time of the Gold Rush, requiring vast capital outlay and technical skills which only large companies could provide. Fortunes were made and lost overnight. Those who became rich and powerful exercised considerable influence on the development of the city.

Transportation services were dominated by a small group of men who owned not only the railroads, but also the network of ferry boats across the Bay, the streetcar routes, and the famous cable car lines running up to the fashionable Nob Hill district.

On April 18, 1906, the Great Earthquake hit San Francisco, destroying the entire area from the waterfront to Market Street. Only a year before this disaster, Daniel Burnham had presented plans to beautify the city with axial boulevards and curving avenues around the hills. The disaster, should have provided the opportunity to restructure the layout of the city, but powerful vested interests restored the rigid grid pattern.

However, San Francisco recovered quickly, and within ten years it had become the shipping capital of the west. In 1915, the city was self-confident enough to host the Panama Pacific International Exhibition on land reclaimed

A TALE OF TWO EARTHQUAKES

The Great Earthquake of 1906 registered an estimated 8.3 on the Richter scale, making it the third most severe of this century. Broken gas pipes exploded, causing fires which raged uncontrolled for three days, destroying entire areas of the city. Of the population of 400,000, it is now reckoned that 3,000 were killed, while 100,000 were left homeless. A tent city for 20,000 was set up in the Golden Gate Park, while others camped on their own plots.

Compared to the 1906 earthquake, the one that took place in 1989 was far less damaging. The quake registered 7.1 on the Richter scale, only one-sixtieth of the force of the earlier one. A total of 63 persons were killed and 3,800 injured. Some 24,000 homes and 4,000 businesses were lost at a total estimated cost of $6 billion. Today's

buildings are better designed for earthquakes, and services are better prepared for emergencies.

San Francisco sits beside the San Andreas Fault, the division between two of the plates of the earth's crust. These move slowly against each other – in 50 million years, San Francisco and Los Angeles, each sited on one of the plates, will meet. The fault does not slip steadily: it sticks for decades at a time, then suddenly lets go, unleashing immense energies, as in Los Angeles in January 1994.

PROCLAMATION BY THE MAYOR

The Federal Troops, the members of the Regular Police Force and all Special Police Officers have been authorized by me to KILL any and all persons found engaged in Looting or in the Commission of Any Other Crime.

I have directed all the Gas and Electric Lighting Co.'s not to turn on Gas or Electricity until I order them to do so. You may therefore expect the city to remain in darkness for an indefinite time.

I request all citizens to remain at home from darkness until daylight every night until order is restored.

I WARN all Citizens of the danger of fire from Damaged or Destroyed Chimneys, Broken or Leaking Gas Pipes or Fixtures, or any like cause.

E. E. SCHMITZ, Mayor
Dated, April 18, 1906.

A postcard shows the Call Building and surrounding ruins in 1906.

from the Bay.

Today San Francisco is regarded as the most beautiful city in the U.S., with rows of 19th-century wooden houses perched on some 40 undulating hills, surrounded by greenery and facing the water on three sides. Topography is closely related to wealth; the rich live higher on the hills.

San Francisco covers an area of 48 square miles on the narrow peninsula alone. The metropolitan district stretches out to the north and east across two spectacular bridges, the Bay and Golden Gate, across the harbor to Marin County and northern California, forming a conurbation known as the Bay Area.

The Golden Gate Bridge was designed by Joseph Strauss in 1930, with a clear span of 4,200 feet between the tall orange towers.

HONG KONG

Chinese in cultural orientation, capitalist in its brashness, and Western in outlook, Hong Kong has defied its ordered Victorian origins and looks with caution toward an uncertain future.

Hong Kong is one of the busiest and most crowded places in the world. Its unceasing bustle is set against a background which is a vivid mixture of British colonial influence – the city still has double-decker buses – traditional Chinese style and hi-tech high-rise. It is significant that even in 1979, when Sir Norman Foster was designing the huge Hongkong and Shanghai Bank building with its revolutionary structure, he consulted a Chinese geomancer, a practitioner of the ancient art of *feng shui,* in order to plan the building so that it faced in an auspicious direction.

A fragrant island

The island of Hong Kong was ceded to the British after their defeat of the Chinese in the First Opium War. A military force under Captain Charles Elliot landed at the western end of the island (now known as Possession Point) in 1841 and raised the British flag.

Hong Kong had a population of no more than 7,500, most living in about 20 villages. There was an excellent harbor at the mouth of the Pearl River, long known to British ships as an anchorage, but the island 8 miles long and 3 miles wide was otherwise barren and uninhabited.

The origin of the name may stem from the word *heung,* meaning "fragrant," in reference to the many kinds of herbs found there. The local name *H'ang Kiang* refers to the "fragrant streams" on the southwestern coast of the island, where ships used to water near a cave and a cascade.

On the north coast, near a fishing village, a tent was pitched for the Government residence. In June 1841, the first land sale took place. Hong Kong became a free port with its own

KEY

☐ *Settlement and coastline in 1840*

▨ *Extent in 1904*

☐ *Reconstruction area*

❶ *Church of St. John*

❷ *Government House*

❸ *Hongkong and Shanghai Bank*

❹ *Victoria Peak*

❺ *Star Ferry Terminals*

❻ *Harbour Tunnel*

❼ *Airport*

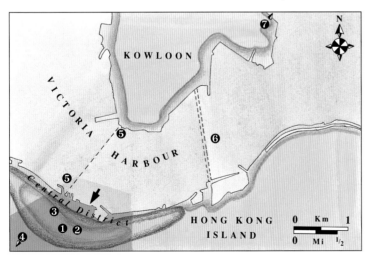

The Hongkong and Shanghai Bank Building (1979–80) by Sir Norman Foster is a symbol of the economic power of this island city.

The reconstruction shows the central district of Hong Kong as seen from the Star Ferry in Kowloon, in the 1920s.

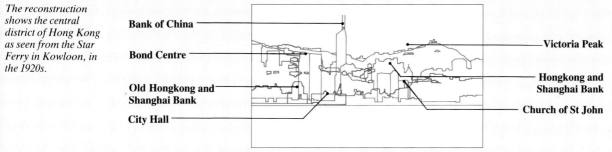

Bank of China

Bond Centre

Old Hongkong and Shanghai Bank

City Hall

Victoria Peak

Hongkong and Shanghai Bank

Church of St John

harbormaster and chief magistrate.

The British government applied all its imperial experience to build Hong Kong into a center of trade and enterprise. Soon, a town called Victoria was laid out with wide streets, and a military road was constructed around the whole island. At first, Western traders remained in Canton. Murders, robberies, and piracy were rife, and dysentery and fever endemic. However, the population grew, from 18,000 in 1846 to 72,000 in 1855, by which time Hong Kong was self-supporting.

At the end of the Second Opium War (1856–60), China was forced to cede the Kowloon ("nine dragons") Peninsula facing the island. In 1898, the New Territories were added on a 99-year lease to Britain. By 1891, the population had reached 221,000, of which 211,000 were Chinese.

By the turn of the 20th century, British rule, supported by the armed forces, civil service,

and experienced merchants, could offer a stable infrastructure for the development of trade, combined with efficient banking, insurance, and shipping services with little bureaucratic interference. In turn, Chinese merchants contributed capital, business skills, and connections with other communities in Southeast Asia, Australia and North America, making Hong Kong a unique financial center.

At the same time, new British companies gathered in the free port of Hong Kong to exploit the lucrative Chinese market, through barter, exchange currencies, and a certain amount of smuggling.

Investment and growth

Britain's free trade policy in Hong Kong encouraged merchants to move where a stable government and a good location offered substantial prospects for commercial growth.

Insurance became essential to the shipping

business, often threatened by typhoons and piracy. The port became the transhipment and distribution center for countries trading with China. By the beginning of the 20th century, opium, which had given rise to the shipping business, was no longer important, and in 1911, Britain agreed to eliminate the trade in Indian opium before 1917.

As Hong Kong's influence increased, so did the development of the town, making use of elements typical of the British Empire. Queen's Road was the main street, extending the whole east–west length of the town and accommodating the principal offices, banks, and shops.

The Church of St. John was set above the waterfront, looking over the harbor to Kowloon in the north. Government House was on one side and Flagstaff House on the other. Close by were the Public Gardens, the Cricket Ground, the Barracks, and parade grounds.

The waterfront buildings were planned in a neoclassical manner adapted to the climate, while the quaysides were designed in a traditional Chinese style. At the rear were the steep streets of Victoria Peak, the most fashionable residential area in town. Here, the imperial merchants, known as *taipans,* built palaces in somber gray tones and planted lush gardens.

The shoreline has been extended by several reclamation schemes from 1843 on. Between 1868 and 1873, the sea front was built up to today's Des Voeux Road. By 1904, further extensions had reached the current Connaught Road, and the present waterfront was completed after World War II.

Difficulties with neighbors

On Christmas Day 1941, Hong Kong surrendered to Japan and, until August 30, 1945, when the Far Eastern Fleet entered the colony, was subject to a repressive occupation.

THE WORLD'S HIGHEST DENSITIES

The ideal density of population and development depends on many factors, including the distance from residential areas to the center of employment, the cost of the site in relation to that of the building, the living patterns of the people, and the range of facilities they may require. The character of the surrounding environment may also be important.

In the city center, most of the population lives in large apartment buildings.

In Hong Kong, more than 80 percent of the people live on less than 20 percent of the land. Large numbers live on sampans and junks, while many thousands occupy makeshift dwellings in shanty towns. Others still lead a semi-rural existence in villages. But the vast majority of the population lives in high-rise buildings in congested urban districts.

Kowloon contains some of the highest population densities in the world – about 660 per acre – but the local population has adapted well to the cramped high-rise accommodation which lies above the garish, glittering storefronts.

The lack of land has necessitated "multi-purpose buildings," in which many facilities are provided in the same structure. Numerous buildings in Hong Kong are owned by several persons or organizations, each also owning a share of the site. Developers undertake long negotiations to acquire sites for redevelopment. This problem has been partly overcome through compulsory purchase by the government authorities, and by the development of new towns on previously unbuilt land.

When the lease on the New Territories runs out in 1997, Britain has agreed to return all Hong Kong, including the parts annexed by treaties, to China. Today the city is being prepared for a certain level of self-rule in time for 1997. Substantial investment is being made in large projects, notably a new airport to take the strain off the existing one, Kai Tak. But it is undeniable that the inhabitants are apprehensive, and many business people have already emigrated.

During the 1950s, emphasis changed from international trade to industrial development, which in turn led to Hong Kong's present world status in financial dealings. Demand for industrial land dominated town plans.

By 1961, the urban population had grown to 2.6 million, with Chinese accounting for more than 82 percent of the total. Up to the 1960s, population growth was absorbed both vertically, through high-rise apartments, and horizontally, mainly around Victoria Harbour. During the 1970s, plans were put forward for decentralization, to be done by creating new settlements in the mainly rural areas. In 1972, the Housing and New Town Programmes were launched as a ten-year project. This considerably redistributed Hong Kong's population outside the main centers.

Kowloon (far left), on the Chinese mainland, was ceded to the British at the end of the Second Opium War.

Kai Tai International Airport in Kowloon, its runway extending into the bay.

NEW YORK

The Manhattan skyline is a symbol of the entire United States. Beneath it, millions of immigrants found the gateway to a new life.

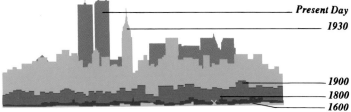

New York is the largest city in the United States, and its commercial and financial center. The city still teems, as it has for centuries, with immigrants from all over the world. Life here is lived faster and louder than in other cities, nonstop 24 hours a day. Manhattan, the oldest of its five districts, is renowned for its soaring skyscrapers, whose beauty belies the purely commercial reasons for their construction. The well-known grid pattern of its streets has an equally commercial origin. Both have been immensely influential in the design of cities in America and elsewhere.

For a few cents an acre

New York's story begins at the mouth of the Hudson River, 230 miles north of Washington, D.C. The river is named after Henry Hudson, who explored the area in 1609.

In 1626, a Dutchman named Peter Minuit made a remarkable deal with the local Algonquin Indians and purchased the whole of Manhattan Island, about 13 miles long and 2 miles wide, for a few trinkets worth no more than $24. The Indians concerned may not even have been from Manhattan. However, once the Dutch felt they had legalized the occupation, they built a permanent settlement on the southern tip of the island, which they called New Amsterdam. A large fort was planned, but in the event the town grew casually, with streets laid out as they were needed.

The Statue of Liberty holds aloft a beacon to enlighten the world – an inspiring image.

New York was the first modern "vertical city."

KEY

- ▢ *Extent 1664*
- ▦ *Extent 1780*
- ▢ *Extent 1850*
- ▢ *Extent 1890*
- ▢ *Reconstruction area*

- ❶ *Wall Street*
- ❷ *Central Park*
- ❸ *New York Tribune Building*
- ❹ *Brooklyn Bridge*
- ❺ *Statue of Liberty*
- ❻ *Chrysler Building*
- ❼ *Empire State Building*
- ❽ *Rockefeller Center*
- ❾ *World Trade Center*

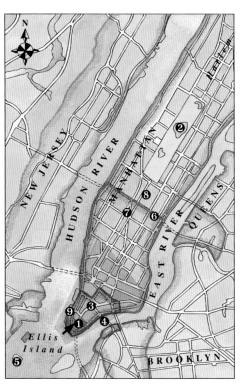

Present Day
1930
1900
1800
1600

The reconstruction shows Battery Park and Wall Street at the southern tip of Manhattan, from New York Bay, 1930s.

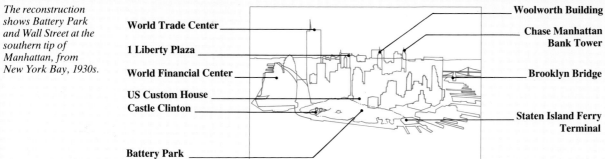

World Trade Center

1 Liberty Plaza

World Financial Center

US Custom House
Castle Clinton

Battery Park

Woolworth Building

Chase Manhattan
Bank Tower

Brooklyn Bridge

Staten Island Ferry
Terminal

The Dutch built a settlement which they called New Amsterdam. The town, shown here in the early 1650s, grew casually with streets laid out as they were needed.

Minuit was succeeded by various governors, the most famous being Peter Stuyvesant (1647–64). New Amsterdam doubled in population and extent and was protected from the British to the north by an encircling wall. Stuyvesant also built himself a farm – in Dutch, *bouwerij* – which was to lend its name to the Bowery district.

Many of the original streets survive today, perhaps the most famous being Broadway, the backbone of Manhattan. This street, originally a Native American path, linked New Amsterdam with estates to the north, as well as early settlements such as Bowery village and Harlem. Broadway now runs for 17 miles, from the tip of Manhattan in the south to Westchester County in the north. Wall Street follows the line of the fortification wall erected in 1653.

The British took over what was a promising trading center in 1664, when the population was a mere 1,500. They renamed it New York. Land not yet allocated to individuals was taken into public ownership. Through the introduction of their system of local government, the

British gained municipal control of the city.

With increasing trade, the city grew rapidly. By 1728, New York extended beyond its original Dutch boundaries, without a clear plan. Growth took place street by street, plot by plot, as landowners decided to turn over farmland to building. The haphazard nature of this development is reflected in the irregular street pattern in the lower part of Manhattan, in contrast to the rest of the island.

During the War of Independence, New York was occupied by British troops, and land speculation was suspended. Many buildings were destroyed by two large fires, and the population halved, from 20,000 to 10,000.

Despite the destruction, New York became the capital of the infant United States from 1785 to 1789, and it was here in 1789 that George Washington was inaugurated as the first President. Trade began again in earnest. By the start of the 19th century, New York was the economic capital of the country, leading to a rapid increase in its population.

The checkerboard city

As a result of the 1782 Act of Confiscation, which took land from those who had sided with the British, and previous Acts dealing with common land, substantial areas were available for development. A Commission was set up in 1807 to prepare a layout of streets and plots. Its plan, put forward in 1811, was a simple grid pattern, without consideration given to the terrain, or civic design, or to the application of planning principles, such as those followed in European cities at that time.

The result was a monotonous pattern of streets, relentlessly stretching as far as the eye could see. Broadway managed not to follow the rigid chessboard pattern and survived along its original course. Wherever it crossed a major thoroughfare, a square was laid out – today's names are Union, Madison, Herald, and Times. Even so, relatively little land was allocated for public service and amenities, particularly open space. By 1890, almost all of Manhattan Island was a vast grid.

According to the Commission's surveyor, the main purpose of this inflexible plan was to

Broadway was a Native American path linking settlements like beads on a string. This view shows the thoroughfare in 1875.

CENTRAL PARK

In 1853, an area of wasteland was acquired by New York City for a large park in the center of Manhattan, between what is now Fifth Avenue and Central Park West. The Commission of Estimate and Assessment offered $2,000 for the winning design in a competition, which was won by Frederick Law Olmstead and his English collaborator Calvert Vaux.

The design for this 843-acre park was highly innovative. There was almost complete separation of traffic, with a system of walkways, bridle paths, and roads. A sunken east-to-west transverse road for commercial traffic was the first example of an underpass, now a common feature in highway design.

By the turn of the century, the park had gained museums and playing fields. In the 1930s, roads and sidewalks were provided to meet the demands of the motor vehicle. Restoration plans in line with the original design began in 1979, re-creating the old sheep meadow and conservatory garden.

Central Park is visited by 15 million people every year. Its irregular plan contrasts with the rectangular site surrounded by straight lines of tall buildings.

facilitate "buying, selling and improving real estate." This speculative land approach to city planning became the model for many other cities in America, for example, Salt Lake City.

A major boost to business and commerce was the completion of the Erie Canal in 1825, providing a waterway trade route from the Atlantic to the Great Lakes, and steam boats plied the Hudson between Albany and New York City. From then on, the population grew rapidly, from 150,000 in the 1820s to almost a million by the 1870s, and 3.5 million by 1900. Brooklyn Bridge, opened in 1885, was the first bridge across the East River. In 1904, the first subway was completed.

New York was also the "gateway to the nation." Between 1855 and 1890, over 7 million immigrants entered the United States through New York – 80 percent of all newcomers (who were mainly Europeans). A further 12 million arrived between 1892 and 1954.

Today New York City has more than 7 million inhabitants, with almost a third foreign-born and half non-white. The city covers an area of 365 square miles, of which nearly 20 percent consists of inland waterways. Of the five boroughs, Manhattan has the highest density, with 1.5 million inhabitants concentrated in an area of 22.6 square miles.

The vertical city

When Elisha Graves Otis, from Yonkers in New York, invented the "safe hoist" in 1852, tall buildings became a practical proposition. In the 1880s, the word "skyscraper" was coined to describe these new structures.

Until the mid-1880s, tall buildings had been limited by the traditional construction method of loadbearing masonry walls. The invention of the girder frame, at first of cast iron, then of steel, allowed building on a new scale. The framework freed walls from their task of carrying the building's weight. They were now simply cladding, serving to insulate and ornament the building. A further step was the invention of air conditioning by Willis H. Carrier in 1902, which solved the tricky problem of ventilating a very large building.

The Tribune Building, 1875.

The stylish Art Deco Chrysler Building, completed in 1930, is probably the most popular skyscraper in the world. At 85 storys, 792 feet, it held the record briefly for the tallest

---

HARLEM

When the Dutch first arrived in New Amsterdam, one of the small villages they established from a group of farms was New Harlem. Up to the middle of the 19th century, the area was still mainly farm land. But with the coming of the New York and Harlem Railroad, the area was ripe for development, attracting well-to-do immigrant families. Here, elegant and fashionable houses were built along tree-lined streets.

When work started on the Lenox Line at the end of the 19th century, speculators built good-quality homes, anticipating that

Constructed in the 1880s, New York's elevated railway

more people would come to Harlem. However, New Yorkers were reluctant to go so far north, and many buildings remained empty. A black speculator bought the empty properties at a low price and rented them to black people from Lower Manhattan. Within a short time, Harlem became a black community.

Today, its reputation is partly as a blighted ghetto and partly as a social and cultural center for black Americans; but in either case, it is a resilient, inward-looking community. Some 10 percent of the city's black population lives in Harlem.

---

building – until the following year, when the Empire State Building (102 storys – 1250 feet) took over the record, only lost in 1974. Its appearance during the Depression was described by the *New York Times* as a "monumental proof to hopefulness." In 1933, a 22-acre site was planned, containing 19

buildings, which created a long mall leading to a pleasant open space at a lower level with an ice rink (in winter) surrounded by stores and cafés. Designed to attract people from surrounding offices, it provided a rare public amenity. This was the Rockefeller Center. The Seagram Building, a mere 39 storys, with

Manhattan's dramatic skyline is a symbol of the triumph of capitalism. The four photographs show the sequence of the

development of Park Avenue, at first on a natural human scale, then increasingly adapted to the demands of the car.

The skyscraper as advertisement – the Empire State Building on a lady's compact.

its well proportioned fenestration in tinted glass and bronze, was built in 1958 and became a landmark in the design of elegant skyscrapers. The 110-story twin towers of the World Trade Center of 1972 reach up 1,453 feet), dwarfing New York's other skyscrapers.

Seen from ground level, tall buildings of varying height can disguise the monotony of excessively long and straight thoroughfares. However, the Pan Am and Helmsley buildings, actually built across Park Avenue, reduce the vista and create an oppressive "canyon" effect. In contrast, the view from the observation platforms on top of the skyscrapers is exhilarating. To the first visitors who eagerly climbed to the top of the Empire State Building, Central Park appeared "a small pasture."

Manhattan's whole is more impressive than its individual building parts. As early as 1909, the Mayor of New York became aware that the city "has a beauty of its own." From a distance, the simple clarity of the dramatic skyline of New York is recognized as a symbol of the prosperity of the entire nation.

GREENWICH VILLAGE

The irregular street pattern on the west side of Greenwich Village (near Perry and Hudson Streets) is attributed to the time in the early 18th century when Sir Peter Warren's estate, consisting of some 300 acres, was sold off in lots of 10 acres. Streets were rapidly laid out, and although the buildings have since been replaced, the street pattern remains.

The Washington Arch, on Washington Square at the center of Greenwich Village.

Washington Square, in the southeast of Greenwich Village, was used as a graveyard, then later as an execution ground for public hangings, and so became a tourist attraction. When the Village became fashionable, wealthy people moved in; the square was regarded as a haven from the yellow fever epidemic of 1822. Later, the square was turned into a military ground and then a park.

In the middle years of the 19th century, the Village attracted such literary figures as Edgar Allan Poe, Walt Whitman, and Mark Twain. The south side of Washington Square was known as "Genius Row." The square is celebrated in the title of a novel by Henry James, dating from 1880.

The Chrysler Building, with its stylish Art Deco design, has remained the most popular skyscraper in the world since it was built in 1930.

PAST VISIONS OF THE FUTURE

Ambrogio Lorenzetti's grandiose vision of Siena in the 14th century shows machiolated towers and palaces, squares and streets, filled with citizens from every walk of life. It was part of a series of frescoes on the "Effects on Good Government in the City and Country" which contrasted good and bad administration.

The vision of the ideal city may be traced back to the philosophers of ancient Greece. Plato wrote in his *Republic* that it must not exceed a size where one citizen could know all the others, at least by sight – an ideal lost in today's huge conurbations, where the pace of change is so rapid that it is often hard to recognize places, let alone citizens. Aristotle described the rectangular grid street layout in his *Politics*; this idea has proved more durable. Hippodamos of Miletus outlined the social order of the city state, dividing the population into three classes.

Systems for cities

Although Roman cities were planned on a rigid grid, the Roman architect Vitruvius Pollio in his *De architectura* described a plan based on a center. He greatly influenced Italian architects of the Renaissance, such as Leon Battista Alberti and Antonio Filarete, who envisaged a *città ideale* with streets of perfectly proportioned buildings radiating from a monumental core. Others, such as Vincenzo Scamozzi and Giorgio Vasari, planned cities on a conventional grid pattern within polygonal fortifications. Leonardo da Vinci devised not only new schemes of fortifications but streets on two levels, anticipating modern city planning.

Although these architects designed many notable buildings, none of their grand schemes was built in its entirety. In 1516 in England, Sir Thomas More devised his ideal society, with much detail of city planning. Realizing that it was an unattainable goal, he called it *Utopia*, meaning "no place."

Amid the haphazard growth and urban squalor of the Industrial Revolution, some benevolent, if paternalistic, industrialists planned ideal villages to improve the lives of their workers. One of the first was the Yorkshire textile magnate Sir Titus Salt, who built Saltaire outside Bradford in 1853. Such communities often included not only housing,

The ideas of Leonardo da Vinci for city planning were based on the requirements of an urban society, rather than on the principles of geometry. His separation of pedestrians and traffic by creating two levels is more akin to concepts of the 20th century than his own Renaissance period.

"Plug-in City," designed by the Archigram Group in the 1960s, expressed a fantastic, impermanent world. Housing units, built to last a few years, could be clipped onto a more durable central structure.

In this study of 1922 (below), Le Corbusier visualized a totally new urban environment, based on a new technology of tall buildings and multilevel highways.

but also parks and places of recreation to keep the workers away from inns and other dens of vice – not entirely an altruistic gesture, as it improved factory output.

Cities in the sky

At the end of the 19th century, Ebenezer Howard refined these ideas into the "garden city," a means of creating a better society. From 1901, the French planner Tony Garnier devised a city on similar lines, published as *Une Cité industrielle* in 1917. Le Corbusier, in *La Ville radieuse* of 1924, proposed a modern Utopia, its inhabitants housed in a formal layout of skyscrapers surrounded by parkland – an ideal which was put into practice after World War II by means of high-rise buildings. Even

the more down-to-earth American Frank Lloyd Wright conceived an entire city in a mile-high skyscraper.

As urban populations burgeoned and technology developed, concepts of the ideal city merged with science fiction. The Archigram Group's "Plug-in City" of the 1960s had urban units which could be clipped onto service cores as required – an idea partly realized in Kuokawa Kisho's "Capsule Tower" in Tokyo, built in 1972.

People have never been satisfied with cities as they are, but it is seldom possible to build one from scratch. The few modern cities that have been built on "greenfield" sites – such as Chandigarh in India, Brasilia in Brazil, and Islamabad in Pakistan – are mostly ceremonial capitals and do not work as communities. The real life of Brasilia, for example,

Buckminster Fuller constantly challenged the imagination, here enclosing central Manhattan in a geodesic dome to create a totally controlled environment.

takes place in the shanty town which has grown up around the immaculately planned center.

Practical development can never be more than piecemeal. Yet as long as architects strive toward an ideal, there is a chance of improving the condition of society.

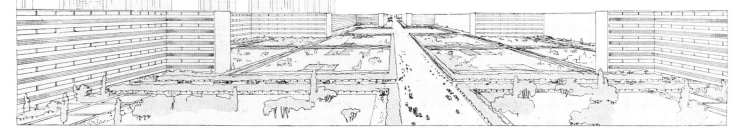

143

PHOTOGRAPHIC CREDITS

l = left, *r* = right, *c* = center, *t* = top, *b* = bottom

Ace 31, 39, 41*l*, 48*l*, 55*r*, 81*l*, 90*b*, 110, 113*b*, 114*t*, 123, 126*l*; Jim Antoniou 7*r*, 11*l*, 81*r*, 84, 140*b*; B & U International Picture Service, Amsterdam 67; La Belle Aurore 15; Photographie Bulloz 142*r*; Robert W. Cameron, San Francisco 79, 95; J. Allan Cash 7*l*, 8*l*, 53, 133*r*; Freda Clinch 82*t*; Moira Clinch 69*tl* & *r*, 90*l*, 125*t*, 133*t*; Colorific! 40*l*; Comstock Photofile 50*r*, 104; Dagnall Worldwide Photo Library 76; C M Dixon 16*l*, 22*b*, 30, 34*r*, 38*l*, 46, 48*t*; et archive 9, 17*l*, 23*t*, 25*l* & *r*, 32*l* & *r*, 33*b* & *t*, 34, 38*l*, 42, 47*l*, *r* & *t*, 48*b*, 60*t*, 63*b*, 70*t*, 74, 88, 89*l*, 91*t*, 102*l* & *t*, 103*l*, 111*r*, 118*b*, 141*tl*, 142*l*; Gemeentelijke Archiefdienst, Amsterdam 64; Michael Helford 105; Angelo Hornak 141*bl*; Hulton Deutsch 41*r*, 111*t*, 112*r*, 113*r*, 132; Image Bank 29, 40*r*; Japan National Tourist Organisation 118*t*; Robin Kerrod 10; Life File 50*l*, 83*r* & *t*, 91*r*, 141*br*; Billie Love Historical Collection 60*r*, 62; Mansell Collection 82*r*; Museo della Civilta', Rome 22*t*; Narodni Museum, Prague 61; State Library of New South Wales 103*t*; Peter Newark's American Pictures 92, 96*l* & *r*, 120, 124*b* & *t*, 125*b*, 127*l* & *r*, 134, 138*l*, 138*l* & *r*, 140*t*; Peter Newark's Historical Pictures 89*r*, 90*r*; Oriental Institute Museum, University of Chicago 6; Pictor 11*r*, 12*r*, 16*r*, 23*r*, 70*r*, 83*l*, 114*b*, 119*c*, *l* & *r*; Pictures Colour Library 73; PowerStock Photo Library 101; Quarto 12*l*, 16*b*, 82*l*; Zev Radovan, Jerusalem 37, 38*tr*; Rex Features 8*r*; British Architectural Library, RIBA 143*b*, *r* & *t*; Spectrum Colour Library 56, 75*t*, 131; Tony Stone Images 24, 59, 63*t*, 75*r*, 87, 97, 106, 113*l*, 126*r*, 139; Hideyuki Tanaka 117; Telegraph Colour Library 21, 38*c*, 45, 69*b*, 137; A. Tjagny-Rjadno/Trip 109; Visual Arts Library 68, 80*r*, 98; Zefa Picture Library 54*l*, 103*r*.

Additional illustrations were supplied by Jim Antoniou; Bedford Square, p. 89, is reproduced by courtesy of London Voice in the *Evening Standard*. We would also like to thank the Royal Geographical Society, London, for their help in preparing this book.

RECONSTRUCTION ILLUSTRATIONS
Kevin Jones Associates 13, 65, 93, 99, 129, 135; Kevin Maddison 19, 27, 35, 43, 51, 57, 71, 85, 107, 121; Janos Marffy 77; Laurence Taylor 115.